Stories That Fit in a Teacup
and Other Things To Sip

A special thank you to Komal Jain for her encouragement and insightful suggestions.

Contents

Something Philosophical

The Mermaid Parade

The Mermaid Parade takes place in Coney Island once a year, in the month of June.

People who attend dress in handmade costumes and celebrate the beginning of summer.

Things typical to the parade are vehicles, floats, and sea creature themes.

A few years ago two friends attended the parade together.

"The weather was unbearably hot," one of them told me. *"The parade was so crowded, and tacky, and a tourist trap, and I'm just happy to be back. It was a zoo."*

"The parade was amazing," said my other friend, *"just magical. Gorgeous women dressed as mermaids, people having fun with their whole families, beautiful blue skies; such a display of creativity and inventiveness. The Mermaid Parade is iconic and I'm so happy I decided to experience it."*

We select our stories. Our stories create our life.

The Glue

I am passionate about life. It's just so interesting how it glares at you, how stories sprout from cracks on the walls that hold me in, short, tight, coiled, green, contained.

I am passionate about stories, how willing they are, how they offer themselves up. Tell people. Tell people what happened. Tell people about me, how I waited for her for hours in the rain.

I am passionate about words. Because without them how would I tell you anything? Maybe through music or math but words are what I was given.

To you, the gift of words. I am not implying that you will be good. I am saying you will be compelled.

Words will always be what you find most urgent.

And language. I love it. It's so fierce. Some people think it's money but it's language that can get you anything. It's language that can make you lose it all.

And love. I'm passionate about love. It's the glue, the connective tissue, the conductor, the thread. It's what strings it all together, what covers everything in glitter, why it all looks resplendent even when it's dark.

4

It's the shimmer, the shimmer that I want to tell you about the most and I don't know if I ever will be able to faithfully convey it, but it's the fact that this is what I choose to die trying to do that confirms that yes. It's this.

This is what I'm passionate about.

I Should Jump

I had a terrible cough. The doctor prescribed a syrup. I took a tablespoon — the amount suggested for a person my age and size — and planned to spend the day home sick.

Shortly after taking the syrup I felt myself detach from my body. I wasn't completely separate — I was sort of floating above it. The feeling was not at all pleasant — it was a form of claustrophobia, like I feel this awful separation from myself and I can't get out. I don't know how to put myself together again.

I walked around my house very slowly, so my body wouldn't be left behind. I looked at things: the photos, the furniture, the cushions, the blankets. Everything looked distant and familiar, like it belonged to someone I used to be.

Look — the people who loved her. The things she owned. Who was she?

I went up the stairs and from the second floor looked down onto the living room. *I should jump*, I thought. Not because I wanted to hurt myself, but because I knew I'd float gently down, like a leaf in the breeze, and it would maybe feel good, help connect the pieces of me that seemed to be drifting.

A part of me — a voice in the back of my mind — thought this jumping off thing was not such a good idea. *Go to bed, Dushka,* she said. *Just go to bed.*

I slept for 18 hours, and when I woke up I called the doctor and described what had happened. *"The cough syrup had codeine in it,"* he said. *"People feel what you felt when they have much larger dosages. You shouldn't be taking opiates. That was not a normal reaction."*

I look back on this incident and remember how terrible it felt to feel unglued from myself, how close I was to causing myself serious harm, possibly dying. It was terrifying.

I have never done recreational drugs. I don't think my body chemistry would react well to anything.

Heartbroken

Last week I attended a big, crowded yoga class.

The teacher began by saying that for many people yoga is a healing practice. That he wanted to dedicate the class to this: an effort directed at mending what was hurt, sprained, wounded or broken.

"This can be a physical injury," he said, *"or a non-physical one like sorrow, anxiety, loneliness.*

"In this class, pay special attention. Take care of yourself. Be loving towards yourself. And send particular care towards whatever you need to heal.

"Now, place both hands on where that place is for you and let's take a few deep breaths."

At this point I sneak a peek. I open my eyes and slowly pan the room.

I'd say 97% of the people in the room had placed both their hands over the left side of their chest.

This is what I want everybody to know today: tread very carefully as you move through the world. Think twice about what you plan to say and do.

Pretty much everyone you come across is desperately trying to mend a broken heart.

Bracelet

Many years ago I was lying on a lounging chair on the beach.

As I extended and relaxed my arms, dipping my fingers into the warm, fine sand directly underneath me, I felt the delicate gold bracelet I was wearing slip clean off my wrist.

I sat up and looked for it but never found it again.

The loss of this bracelet perplexed me. It was a smooth slide rather than a throw or a toss. It was the equivalent of gently setting it down.

It should be right here.

It was gone.

Last night I had a vivid dream. I was lying comfortably with my hands folded over my chest and the bracelet, that I have not thought of in decades, was on my wrist.

I am not a dream interpreter and don't really believe dreams carry hidden messages.

I do think it's very beautiful that I am at a place in my life where my subconscious is certain I have found something I thought I had lost forever.

Nothing in Common

Strangers. You *feel* you have nothing in common, but just because you feel something doesn't make it true.

You are both human, this stranger and you. You are both fallible. You have both at one time or another felt powerless.

You know what's true for both of you? Something is making you suffer.

You both have questions you cannot answer and have both at some point looked up at the sky and wondered if it's going to rain.

You have both experienced waiting for something that does not happen, have both felt surprise, pleasure, loneliness, hunger, thirst, desire.

You have both been hurt by someone you thought would never hurt you, have both been disappointed in someone who once filled your heart, have both been isolated and felt certain you had no one to talk to.

Maybe at that very same time you felt this certainty you both had someone out there thinking *"But, you have me"*, because many, many times our sense of aloneness is a lie.

But, back to the stranger. You are probably both standing or sitting in the same place.

Turn around. Look at him. Say hello and give him a nod.

What makes you the same is much more than the things that make you different.

Metal Box

Every day (or almost every day) I somewhat willingly step inside a small, flammable, flimsy metal box loaded with gasoline.

Then, I strap myself in and speed alongside other small, flammable, flimsy metal boxes.

During this time, I am at the complete mercy of other people's actions, maneuvers, judgment, calculations, egos, mood and mental state, all of which I have no control over and a minimal ability to predict.

Driving terrifies me.

Staple Gun

Burning Man is a place for catharsis, for self-search, for exploration, and for beauty. It's also a place of worship.

Every year a temple is designed and erected, and people come with things to revere, to adore, to say goodbye to, to burn.

In a place of elated celebration, The Temple is sacred and peaceful. The day of The Temple Burn marks the end of Burning Man every year.

When you walk inside this structure its walls are covered in graffiti, signs, paper, letters, envelopes. Each one is a story, a heartbreak, its own intimate ceremony.

Two years ago, a friend of mine arrived at The Temple intending to do something in observation of his father's recent death.

He had written a letter for him on a piece of paper he attempted to secure to The Temple wall with duct tape.

At Burning Man, fine silt covers everything. Duct tape loses its stickiness immediately.

My friend is standing there, mourning, heartbroken, struggling with the tape and the letter and thinking there is no way he will ever manage to stick it to the wall.

13

That's when someone taps his back and in classic Burning Man spirit hands him a staple gun.

My friend claims this staple gun is the best gift he has ever received.

He, in fact, returned to Burning Man a year later and walked into The Temple a couple of days before it was supposed to burn, handing a staple gun to anyone who was struggling to affix their letter to the wall.

He held stranger after stranger in his arms and cried.

He says it's the best thing he has ever done.

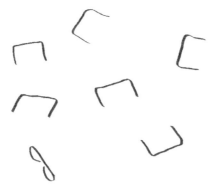

Interference

I had plans, clear and straight and organized. They were good, I think. They made sense. They were designed to get me where I wanted to go.

That's when he came along.

He was by every possible definition a distraction. I found him entertaining, he disordered me, diverted me, disturbing my original plans with his tendency to show interest in me.

At first it felt catastrophic. I tried to resist. Then, well. It would be rigid, I decided, to return to what I originally thought I wanted to do.

It would be better to give myself to the chaos implicit in his arrival.

I mean, what if this was a gift?

Now, I had no way to know where I was headed, felt bewildered instead of determined, was worried I might be frittering away my time.

This is my wish to you. May every plan you carefully design experience at least minor interference.

What if life is not in what we design but in what arrives to show us there will always be a better option?

What if the forging of our spirit lies in something that disarrays instead of in something that allows us to continue, undisturbed, unamused, unbaffled?

As scary as it may be, as befuddling, as painful, I'd rather be disoriented. I'd rather be lost than found. It's when I happen upon the best possible things.

Old Wound

I have a friend who is the oldest of three children. The other two are identical twins.

My friend is keenly aware of the fact that she always feels left out.

I prefer to spend time with small groups of people rather than large ones. This gives me the chance to really talk. If I organize a get-together with common friends I make sure she is included.

The way things affect people is related to old wounds and to where they come from.

Their job is to learn how to untangle their programming in order to suffer less.

From us a little kindness can go a long way.

Begin Again

When I was in my early teens I read a book by Milan Kundera titled *The Book of Laughter and Forgetting*. I liked it so much I proceeded to read all his books.

Twenty years later I picked up one of these books looking for a specific thing he had written about the past's ability to shift. We consider the past immutable, and I wanted to find exactly how he had phrased this very interesting counterargument.

In looking for the quote I began re-reading the book and realized I was interpreting every word differently. How could this be the same book?

I realized the book had not changed, but I had.

This made me feel overwhelmed. Wow. If I change to the point of not recognizing what I read, then that means I have read nothing.

When all questions are answered, we will have to begin again.

Two Minds

I frequently wonder what would happen if I returned home one evening to find me already there.

Would I be living my life? If so, where would that leave me?

How would I feel, seeing me at the door?

We would look at each other as if in front of a mirror, but look. Only I raise my hand.

After some time, the glitch would correct itself and we'd return to one body.

Except that now I'd know why I tend to feel conflicting things and why I am so often of two minds.

What Is It About People That's So Fascinating to You?

I hand him the chocolate bar and he sits down to unwrap it.

He takes care not to tear the gold foil it comes in, gently unfolds, then peels back the edges.

He pulls out the chocolate and breaks a row, gives it to me. I put it in my mouth and let it melt before engaging my teeth.

It's excellent chocolate.

"I love this gold foil," he is saying. He turns it over in his fingers, lays the sheet down on the kitchen counter. He's completely absorbed, runs his nail over every millimeter. He is detailed and systematic and obsessive, holds up a perfect gold rectangle.

"Doesn't this strike you as incredibly valuable?"

Before his arrival there would have been no ceremony. I would have torn open that chocolate bar, chewed on it while doing other things.

I would have never known about the existence of this prized, heavy for its size, glinting lamina. It would have ended up crumpled and thrown in the trash. Not forgotten. Undiscovered.

This is what fascinates me about other people.

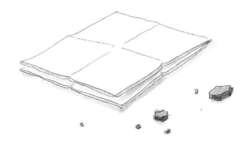

I Want

Most wants are misdirected.

I want ice cream because it's cold and creamy but really I want to be soothed because I'm nervous about where my life is going and ice cream is easier than figuring out what it is that I need to do to not be a cyclical catastrophe.

I want a big bowl of crunchy, salty things but really I'm just tired and what I want is to unwind and give my brain a break and feel like I have a place to set myself down.

I want clothes and shoes and shiny things but really my closet is already full and what I want is something that addresses this emptiness and absence of beauty.

I want a lover and a hotel room and an afternoon out of time but really what I want is to go back to when things were simpler and maybe to feel pleasure in the place of all this jagged loneliness and complexity.

My brain tells me she wants something because it's easier to want that than to identify — and quench — the want that is real.

Martín

By Dushka Zapata
Drawings by Dan Roam

My friend Martín grew up on a street lined with furniture stores.

Sometimes he'd peek in through the windows.

His dream was to play hide and seek inside one of those stores. He'd crouch behind a couch, maybe. Or under a cushion.

After playing hide and seek, he'd spend the night curled up on the most plushy chair.

Today, Martín could throw himself a furniture-store hide and seek party. I find this thought deeply satisfying. Like a writing nook in a treehouse. Like a big swing in my living room.

There is so much we can't fix, but the adults we've become can get the children we once were what we dreamed of.

Maybe this is how we repair
what must be an increasingly
fragmented multiverse.

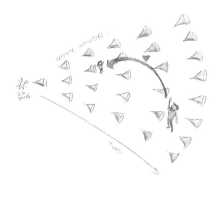

Philosophical Everyday Things

A light bulb. It really has a way of flooding a dark room with light.

Or, a sandwich and its knack for satisfying deep hunger.

An empty purse to remind you of how little you need.

A cushion as an invitation to sit and breathe.

A child who follows you around asking why. And why. And why.

A book as a window into what someone else thinks.

A notebook as a window into what you think.

Comfortable shoes to begin your thousand mile journey.

Planet in My Pocket

If I could fit a celestial body in my pocket it would have to come with its motion and its tilted, wobbly orbit, its unique trajectory and maybe a satellite or two.

It would sit there, small and heavy, complete with its atmospheric pressure and chemical composition, its seasons and that patient, steady migration around a sun.

I'd hold its horizons, its oceans, its deserts and skylines, its cities and forests, its arctic and darkness and its galactic notion of time.

Maybe someday in millions and millions of years I'll find a planet to shrink and carry in my pocket.

Maybe I exist within what a cosmic, curly haired woman carries in hers.

Is Taco Bell Authentic Mexican Food?

Taco Bell is about as close to Mexican food as we are from Icarus, a star in a distant spiral galaxy.

It takes the light from Icarus 9 billion years to reach us, which means that it's not just that it's far, or in an entirely different galaxy, but that by the time you see it the universe has aged and has become something other than what it once was.

Body Parts

I'm glad I have eyes so I can sometimes close them. They were made to see, but at least a hundred times a day I use them to not.

And, was my nose meant for smelling or for nuzzling? If it was meant only for smelling then alas, I love to use it abnormally.

I carry tension in my shoulders. I don't think they were intended for that. They were meant for strength, not stress. Not the weight of the world.

I use my head for nodding and shaking. It was designed to carry my brain, but I instead use it to agree/disagree. Do I want that? Yes. Yes, I do. And, no.

I am a contradiction, and so are you.

I don't know what hair was intended for. To keep my head warm? I use it for flash. Look at it. It's so curly.

I use my chest to feel it expand. To house a swell of well-being. I can't anticipate its arrival and as such have resolved to always be ready. Here we are, my roomy, roomy chest and I.

My legs and feet were meant to carry me but sometimes I lie near a wall so I can put them up against it. I don't know if they were meant to be higher than the rest of me but sometimes I want to give them a break. Thank you. Thank you for taking me to all the places we go.

Puzzle

I have a friend who told me she and her family have become positively obsessed with puzzles.

"Dushka, you open the box to find two thousand pieces of something you can't really make sense of. How will this work? How will it ever come together? How will we solve this? And you don't think that you can and one piece at a time you see an image emerge."

One piece at a time chaos becomes order.

I think puzzles show our brains that even if we don't know how, we will piece by piece come out of this.

If you are living through a problem you don't know how to solve, work on a puzzle.

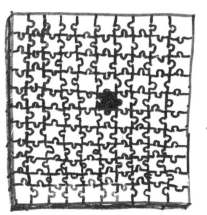

ONE DAY, ALL WILL
BE CLEAR.

So You Can See It

Perfection implies a seamlessness, something consistent, immaculate and exact.

I wonder sometimes if I am surrounded by things so perfect and right that they are indiscernible.

If something perfectly matched the color of the sky and you looked up would it not be invisible?

The reason everything is flawed is because that is the only way we can perceive it.

Why Do People Say, "Be Careful What You Wish For"?

When I was a little girl what I wished for was candy. *Someday,* I used to tell myself, *I will be an adult and buy and eat all the candy I want.*

I wished my parents would not get a divorce. I lived in a house at war and when that divorce came through I realized it was the best thing they could have done for all of us.

When I was a bit older I wished I was popular. I felt like everyone knew how to do something I didn't know how to do. Instead of finding myself at the center of all the bustle and the action and the fun, I found myself.

I wished I could make him love me. Is there pain equivalent to loving someone who doesn't love you back? But I didn't, because I couldn't. What I learned was to find the freedom in walking away from anyone who doesn't feel about me the way I feel about them.

I have wished for many, many good things. Pleasure. Belonging. Love. Peace. But good things and their delivery have more than one dimension. Wishes come with consequences. It's not getting what we once wished for that reveals the price we would have paid.

Be careful what you wish for. Even more than that, don't let all the wishing distract you from the incalculable wealth of what you already have.

Monster

There is a monster underneath the bed, terrified of the child sitting on it.

I hope this kid never confirms I am here.

What if the kid thinks I'm evil? What if the kid thinks I'm going to hurt them?

What if they don't know that I am here to protect them from their own nightmares?

I am scared of this kid.

I've been grazed by arms hanging off this bed, feet hanging off the bed, by an upside down head with disheveled hair hanging off the bed, and have never, not once, given this kid any reason to think I would harm them.

I worry humans assume so many unfounded things about me, and they have never even met me.

Insignificant

There is something beautiful, reverential and deeply peaceful about being reminded of my own insignificance. I feel this when I look out into the ocean, when I go to a museum and see a beautiful object made thousands of years before I existed, when I look up at the stars.

Making another person feel this way — rather than myself — is a different proposition. It means I deliberately make you feel unimportant, measly, small, inferior.

I would not want to do that to anyone.

Wondering

We don't know if we exist.

Wondering — pondering — if we do or don't is a very deep, very human thing to do.

The French philosopher Descartes proposed that *"we could not doubt our existence while doubting"* meaning that the fact that he doubted was proof that he existed. (*"Cogito ergo sum"*)

To put it in other words, if I'm sitting here wondering if I exist it must mean I do, because otherwise who is doing all this wondering?

The fact we can't be sure of this fundamental thing tangles my brain up with both its wonder and its beauty. Wonder and beauty are how I confirm my existence.

How Do Ideas Feel?

Some ideas feel like fear or apprehension or dread.

Some feel like awe.

Some feel like water, slowly brought to a roiling boil.

Some ideas feel like a bolt of lightning slicing across a pitch dark sky.

Some feel like a taste of sugar after drinking something bitter.

Some feel like tripping, like a stumble, like falling over.

Some feel like being startled, stunned, taken aback.

Some feel like floating in a tub of salty water.

Some feel like placing the last piece of a large, confusing puzzle.

Some feel like I just managed to untangle what I thought was a forever-knot.

Some feel like witnessing muddy, slimy water turn into water you can drink.

Some feel like a hot air balloon.

Some feel like jumping off a cliff.

The Taste of Chocolate

You're alone. It's kind of cold in here. You're shivering, and you're missing someone you have not seen in weeks. You wish you could teletransport yourself to wherever they are.

The doorbell rings.

This person you've been missing is outside. They are smiling. They step in and put their arms around you.

You're standing there, enveloped by this person's arms, and you can feel the heat of their skin through their clothes. It permeates right through to your chest and feels so good, it's closer to safety than it is to temperature, closer to happiness than to warmth.

And that's what chocolate tastes like.

Am I Too Old To Play With Legos?

When I was a kid — and I don't mean 13, but rather around 6 — I loved to write. It created an alternate world for me. When I was writing, time did not exist.

It was all I wanted to do.

Which is weird, because over the years, I lost it.

I lost writing to life, I guess. I went to school, made friends, got busy, and got a job. I wrote a bit — in diaries I locked, in notebooks I threw in drawers, in letters I sent off and never saw again.

My writing, dispersed, dissipated, banished.

One day I found myself in a life I couldn't believe was mine. I was in a relationship that wasn't working, in a job that was sucking my soul out of me, grieving the recent death of a person so close to me I think I died on that day too.

For reasons that were mostly a coincidence, I picked writing back up.

It felt like I was dying of thirst and someone handed me a tall glass of clean water. I could not put it down.

I set everything aside to write — everything. I quit my job. I ended my relationship. I moved to a new place — a small apartment that seemed designed for someone who wanted to write.

I wrote fifteen books, one every six months, one right after the other.

Those books are evidence of me figuring myself out: my sadness, my loss, my patterns, my mistakes. Answers to my life questions.

As I wrote those fifteen books, time passed out in the real world.

In that time, my entire life righted itself.

Why am I telling you this?

Because — and I state this with urgency, with certainty — the key to everything, the answers to all the things we desperately look for and cannot seem to find, are all in the things we for some reason decided we were too old to do.

THE ANSWERS WE SEEK ARE IN ALL THE THINGS WE NEVER OUTGREW.

It's Real

Reality is a trap. It's an illusion. Reality is not what happens. It's not how you interpret what happens. It's the angle you choose to believe.

Imagination is instead possibility. It's reach. It's creation.

Every time you can, defy reality. Disbelieve it. And remember this: Imagination is the only thing that's real.

I Can See You

Everything you do — everything — is a reflection of your personality.

The way you wake up in the morning and stretch, or not. How you deal with the reluctance of getting out of a warm bed to face an often cold world. Aaaah. It's so bracing. So invigorating, this cold.

Your personality is expressed in what you eat and what you drink and in if you like that drink so hot you have to wait before you can take the smallest sip.

It's in the choices that you make. It's in your irritability, your discipline, your vigor, your verve or the utter absence of these things.

Your tendency to hesitate before you talk or the way you blurt things out because you can't not.

Your need to process something before you are willing to express it. In your willingness. It's even in your willingness.

It's in the poetry evident in the way you walk and in the lack of poetry in you feeling total frustration. If anything lacks poetry it's that, isn't it?

45

It's in how clean, clear, crisp, harsh everything looks through fury. Never. I have never been this lucid.

Your personality leaves messy, sloppy — or maybe precise, defined — fingerprints all over everything you do that is visible to others. Your perspective. Your impressions. The questions you decide you want to answer. The answers you deem worth leaving your comments in.

You are — inescapably, ineludibly — in everything you do.

Maybe I can't see all of you in each thing, but in each thing I can see you.

Rock Collection

Imagine a truck driver who drives to pay the bills and clear his mind driving across the starlit night but who uses his trips to collect rocks from different places.

He is happiest when he organizes his rock collection, this road warrior/amateur geologist.

There is no money in these rocks that I find around highways everywhere but they fill my heart. What is this rock collection for? I don't know, but it's here that I find myself.

Truck driving pays the bills and also provides access to all these rocks that come from such different topographies.

It's OK for your job to be in one place and your passion in another.

They can come together in unexpected ways and serve each other.

Cumulus Nimbus

I love clouds.

In particular I love *cumulus nimbus* and their outrageous, hard to believe, often extra fluffy shapes.

One day a friend who did not know this about me invited me to his apartment. When I walked in I noticed photos of these very clouds papered his walls.

I learned he spent his Sundays strolling, lying on the grass, photographing the sky with a manual (rather than digital) camera and developing each one himself.

I was enthralled.

Other people there with us that evening barely batted an eye but I instead walked around, neck craned, ogling each photo and then taking in their collective effect.

"Interesting" is not an objective value. It is relative — a matter of preference and taste.

To someone you might have nothing to say.

Another will be transfixed by your silence, or your modesty, or your smile, or the endearing way you look down and shrug and confess you don't have anything to add.

Multiverse

If the universe is infinite and ever-expanding, and time is infinite, then it stands to reason that it's possible that there is in fact an infinity of universes, both different and the same as ours.

Each of these universes have their own infinity, their own galaxies and constellations. People there look up (or maybe look down) on skies that are different and the same as ours. They have laws of physics that are just like ours and completely different. Collections of particles that replicate ours, or collections of particles we cannot even conceive of.

Some people believe that so many things had to happen exactly the way they happened to result in life as we know it today that the existence of another identical universe is unlikely.

Other people think that in a world of infinite combinations it's only logical that this combination has happened and will happen again, or combinations that are only slightly different.

Another you, exactly as you are, reading this answer, written by another me. You, a version of you who has made different decisions and ended up in a very different place, smaller, darker.

You, accomplished, in possession of everything you've ever dreamed of and perfectly happy.

You, in possession of everything you've ever dreamed of, wondering why it still feels you haven't found what you want.

You, thinking of you. You, somewhere out there, wondering if there is another universe where you exist, exactly as you exist today, thinking how incredibly, unbelievably fortunate that version of you would have to be for her improbable existence to even be possible.

Wow

Did you know the oceans are illuminated? There is light and glow and glimmer everywhere, even in the deep.

We live on an incandescent planet that offers multichromatic displays of light no matter where you go.

There are world authorities on this phenomenon — called bioluminescence — who take a boat way out to sea and claim to witness a starry night sky and equally sparkling waters.

We don't yet fully understand the extent of this quality, but it's a fact that there is light even in the darkest places, even in places we have never before ventured into.

I mean, wow.

Creator

The woman is standing on the flimsy metal balcony, looking out onto a spectacular, moonlit view of a city that for centuries has remained unchanged.

No, wait. That is not a woman. That is a man. He is tall and shirtless. His hair is still wet and he's wrapped a towel around his waist.

And no wonder that city has remained unchanged for so long: he has a view of another planet, one that was abandoned and left intact and now belongs to him.

He has a lot on his mind. He has everything he could possibly want and wonders why he still feels so restless, why he cannot sleep through the night, why he thinks of her even after all this time.

If his own planet is somehow not enough, then maybe what he is looking for cannot be found anywhere out there.

The story above began with a woman. I changed her to a man. I took off his clothes. I switched the scene to a different planet. I peered into his thoughts. I exposed his feelings for a woman he irretrievably lost many years ago.

I can do whatever I want because I am a writer and in any world that I conjure I am the creator.

A Good Villain

An interesting villain is not an "other". He is not darkness but is instead like me, almost like me.

I mean completely different, but, well. I understand.

What you want to do is horrifying so how is it that I feel empathy? Why am I rooting for you? How did you do that?

An interesting villain is suave, sophisticated, knowledgeable. It's perfectly perverse that you know what wine to pair with the fava beans and that friend you're having for dinner.

An interesting villain is good. Somehow, underneath all of that. He is redeemable, can be saved from himself and maybe I can be the savior.

A good villain does not expend effort but rather derives pleasure from evil. It's with glee that he calibrates how he will vaporize me; with sheer delight and a chuckle that he *trademarks* the inevitable, inescapable conclusion.

Yeah, everybody dies.

What's the Most Unusual Thing You Are Thankful For?

There is a woman I work with who I really like. Our collaborations are always joyful and fortunate. A few months ago she told me *"today is my four year anniversary at the company."*

I remember thinking *"I don't know what I was doing four years ago, but someone was interviewing her, and she was accepting the offer that would later result in us working together. Four years ago I was minding my own business and had no idea that it was my lucky day."*

This led me to considering all my lucky days that I have been oblivious to.

The day — way before I was even born — that the new boy moved into the neighborhood. He'd come home early and walk his dog. This is how he met her. The two of them would get married and have a baby who would grow up to be my boyfriend and would mark my life.

Think about the people you've met, the warm soft coat you wrap yourself with, the delicious things you eat, anything that grants you a measure of solace or pleasure.

Now think about this: You were busy with who knows what and at the same exact time everything was coming together, just for you.

I am grateful to all the astounding good fortune I am in possession of that I had never before considered.

The Bus

There is a gorgeous man standing next to me on the bus. He's so tall he's hunched over so his head doesn't hit the ceiling.

There are people around me reading real books instead of devices (can you see her over in the corner, sitting in the sun?).

A woman is crying on the phone telling someone about the fight she had with her boyfriend this morning.

Last week I realized I had stopped taking the bus to work because Uber pool is so darn convenient.

But, the bus is full of stories.

Family

I was born in Mexico, to a Mexican father and an American mother. The instant I came into the world my mother spoke to me in English.

I grew up in a Spanish speaking country, speaking Spanish with everyone, including my father, my siblings and everyone around me. But when my mother spoke to me, and when I replied, it was in English.

This to me was invisible, "normal", until I went to school and people struggled in English class. *Why are you struggling? Can't you just speak it?*

I got English for free, and I don't just mean I didn't pay any money for it. I mean I never expended any effort in picking it up, learning it, reading in it, writing in it, expressing myself in it.

As luck would have it, speaking English fluently granted me a huge advantage in school but also when I began interviewing for jobs, when I was employed by an international company, when I ended up writing in English, for a living and for the joy of it.

It's no exaggeration to say English was a gift, and that it marked the trajectory of my life.

I think it's this sense that I got it for free that motivates me to spend so much time tending to it.

Upvotes and Likes

On a bleak, dark, overcast, windy day I am going to take all my upvotes and my likes and stitch them together with iridescent, prismatic, rainbow string.

I'll do so in softly tapered polychromatic patterns.

Then I will carefully wrap up my creation and take it to a grassy bluff overlooking a frothy, unsettled ocean.

I'll fly it — like a kite — and watch the flapping, undulating contrast of its gossamer fabric against a stormy sky.

It will remind me that anything gray, even something as vast as the concave expanse of sky, can be generously streaked with color.

Aliens

Have you heard about slime molds?

Slime molds are single cell organisms that can, by joining other slime molds (for example, when they are looking for food) form a multicellular organism.

When they come together they move as if they were one body and can change the shape and the function of any of its parts.

This thing shapeshifts.

They can produce spores so that an animal, an insect or even the wind can carry them somewhere else.

If you separate a slime mold it finds its way back. This organism can re-form itself, can learn, can predict conditions that will not favor its survival, can make decisions, can find the most nutritious food, can distribute food to different parts of itself, can create networks — it can navigate a maze.

Slime molds can think and have no brain.

It can remember.

I don't know if aliens have come to Earth. I can tell you that stranger, more out of this world things happen here.

Exercise in Fiction

I had just died.

Maybe this was why the scene looked so impossibly vivid:
my red raincoat bright against that gray day; my body, inert,
stretched out on the wet grass, the lined notebook still in
my hand.

I had never seen me from outside myself. The high curves of the
arches of my bare feet. The scars on my shins from learning how
to ride a bicycle so many years before. My wide, fanned out
black skirt, the one we bought together back when things were
different to the way they became at the very end.

And my hair. Look at it. The long, corkscrew tendrils around
my head.

We will all die. You will too. I don't know why we still regard it
as such a tragedy.

Revenge

I will get back at you for every priceless thing you have
given me.

I will rearrange the atoms in the atmosphere around you until
you begin to wonder if maybe the whole universe is conspiring
in your favor.

Grass

I like lying on the grass in the sun. I feel myself settle in, feel time slow down, become a spectator instead of a frantic participant.

I look at people lying on the grass around me, coax pups to come say hello, observe treetops swaying against the sky, examine blades of grass and their unsuspected, miraculous complexity.

I often bring a book but rarely open it. I want to always have a towel with me but never remember it. I aspire to have a picnic but don't organize it. It's usually me and a sweatshirt I take off and spread down.

If I go lie on the grass with him we lie alongside each other, hold aimless, goal-less conversations that meander, touch fingertips, touch toes, touch noses. I leave feeling electric, like connection has finally been reestablished.

Even if I just spend half an hour alone on the grass, I walk away with the sense I just returned from a long vacation. My brain feels rebooted, my body grounded, my clothes covered in bits of dry grass.

Is Norse Mythology Better Than Greek?

Mythology is a collection of stories and beliefs. Countries have it. People have it. Families have it. Individuals have it.

No mythology is better or worse than another. Think of it this way instead: without our stories there is no memory, no chronology, no poetry, no glue.

If you took me and removed all the stories I've ever heard, all the stories I've ever told, all the stories I've ever believed, you would be left with a pile of dust.

Pygmalion

Pygmalion was disenchanted with women. He didn't understand them, often felt hurt and frustrated, and gave up on relationships. He was through with love.

Embittered, he retreated into his studio. He was a sculptor — an artist, not a king — and spent his days in his own company, carving marble.

One day he began working on the sculpture of a woman. As he did so, he felt a spark inside of him. He knew what this was: inspiration.

He focused all his creative energy and passion on this sculpture. He put to use all his talent, all his skill, his loneliness, his despair, his dejection; and his care, his heart, his love.

He put into the sculpture all the things he had to give that had nowhere else to go.

This sculpture — the one he chipped and chiseled and polished from a single block of marble — became the most beautiful woman he had ever seen.

He fell in love with her.

As he worked on his creation the polishing became caressing. The detailing became stroking. The chiseling became kisses. He ran his mouth against her neck. He bought her clothes and dressed her. He laid flowers at her feet.

One day, the goddess of beauty and love, Aphrodite, noticed all this activity. She noticed the care he put into the creation of this sculpture, noticed how he treated her, and certainly noticed her beauty. She could not help but reward Pygmalion's dedication with what he wanted the most.

That evening, Pygmalion arrived in his studio and got up on a step stool to kiss his creation. As he gently placed his human lips on her full, curved, cold stone ones, he felt them move, grow warm, move around his. He felt her arms embrace the small of his back. Under his fingers he felt the vein in her neck pulse with — life.

She was alive, and her name was Galatea.

What Is "Ariadne's Thread"?

Greek mythology is wondrous — full of twists and turns and intrigue and complexity, replete with Gods who act like mortals and mortals who act like Gods.

Once, there was a king named Minos. He had a monster — half bull, half man — living inside a labyrinth and this labyrinth was so convoluted and expertly designed that no one ever got out alive.

Except Theseus did, because Ariadne, the daughter of Minos, helped him get out. How? By giving him thread he could unravel as he walked into the labyrinth. When you need to come out, she said, retrace your steps by following this thread back out.

But, wait.

Do you know why Minos had this Minotaur? Because Zeus impregnated his wife, and the Minotaur was the result.

Did you know the identity of one of the many humans the Minotaur devoured? Androgeus, the son of Minos.

Do you know what Theseus did once Ariadne went behind her father's back to help him? He abandoned her — got on a boat and left her behind, never to return.

Also, before embarking on this dangerous adventure that would almost certainly result in his death, Theseus promised his dad he would change the sails on his boat from black to white so that his dad could see from afar if he had succeeded.

But, his triumphant success caused him such excitement he forgot all about changing the sails. His dad, Aegeus, saw from afar the black sails, believed his son had died and in total despair jumped into the ocean to his death. That's why to this day it's called the Aegean Sea.

And, do you know who designed that most intricate, most deadly of labyrinths? That was Daedalus, who was later held prisoner on a beach with his son, Icarus. They escaped when he designed wings for them, and Icarus was so out of his mind about flying that he flew too close to the sun, melting the wax that held his wings together.

And, do you know the origin — the etymology — of the word "clue"? A clue is whatever gets you closer to the solution of a problem, and it comes from "clew", the thread Ariadne gave to Theseus, in a defiant, fruitless act of love.

Tartarus

According to Greek Mythology, in the very beginning, before the existence of light, there was a force, a deity called Tartarus — a first existing entity from which light and the Cosmos were born. Other comparable forces were Earth, Night and Time.

Much later, Hades became the underworld, comparable to what we today conceive as hell. Hades was ruled by Hades and his wife Persephone and their realm had five subterranean rivers running through it which divided it into regions.

The lowest region of Hades was called Tartarus. This was where the most terrible, ferocious monsters were sent, and the worst possible criminals.

Cronus imprisoned the cyclopes in Tartarus, as well as Hecatonchires, a hundred armed monster. Typhon was also a prisoner of Tartarus, as was Apollo (until Zeus freed him).

To give you a sense of how low Tartarus is, you would have to drop a bronze anvil from heaven. It would take nine full days to reach the Earth. Then, from here, another nine days to reach Tartarus. Tartarus is as far from the Earth as the Earth is from the sky.

Hints Everywhere

Have you ever watched a movie for the second time to realize that all along it was fraught with hints that clearly pointed towards what would happen next?

I bet life is like that.

I wish I could live twice just so I could see.

What Fruit/Food or Anything Edible Surprised You?

Coffee and olives.

I'm surprised by things like coffee beans or olives.

Coffee: *I can't eat this, but maybe if I harvest it, dry it, roast it, grind it and brew it, I can drink it. And, wait! What about a little milk and sugar?*

Olives: *I can't eat this, but if I harvest it, clean it, cure it, brine it, flavor it and wait, then I can eat it. And if I press it, I get oil, and I can use that to sauté things and make them more delicious!*

I guess I am less surprised by the fruit itself and more by our limitless ingenuity, in particular when it comes to eating once inedible things.

Delusional

A man gets on the bus.

He's wearing a smart, very dusty old suit and gold shoes. He is pacing around, restless, deranged, loudly addressing the bus as if we all worked for him. He's getting agitated. The last quarter did not go well so we are being reprimanded.

While this is happening, a guy sitting next to me is wearing AirPods and talking loudly on the phone.

I am irritated by all this activity because I am taking notes in an effort to prepare for my morning meeting.

Suddenly it becomes really hard to tell which one of us is the most delusional.

Gray

Don't believe anyone who claims gray is a neutral. Look at it. The hue has authority.

Gray manages to be both strong and understated, calming and solid. It's a stand up color, subtle, circumspect and conscientious, correct and impartial, trustworthy and upfront.

It goes with everything.

Gray is not flashy or flaunting or jazzy or glaring or conspicuous. It's instead restful. I find it to be the only color I never tire of, which is why it's the one I wear most frequently.

Dirty Sticker

Sometimes I repeat a word so many times it looks funny and loses its meaning and just sits there doing nothing.

Banana banana banana banana

I find it hard to believe I ever used it to convey anything.

Similarly, a very familiar person can suddenly seem alien to me. Who is this man standing in my kitchen? Do I even know him at all?

And, my family members. What a completely arbitrary collection of strangers. Is it not somewhat of a fluke that we ended up being related?

I stand up and walk around and stare for a long time at objects around my house. Once valuable to me, precious, they are now debris, similar to the ones I walk right past at a garage sale.

Reality sometimes feels like a dirty sticker that is peeling off at the edges.

My own breath is the antidote, a small gesture of kindness, a walk among tall trees with gigantic systems of roots that I am certain exist but will never see.

Something That Feels
Like Eavesdropping

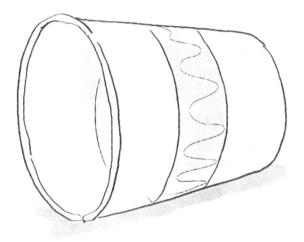

Elevator

Conversation I overheard in an elevator that you really don't want to overhear in an elevator:

Guy 1: *Right after this we are going to the police.*

Guy 2: *Why?*

Guy 1: *Because, dude. You have to turn yourself in.*

On the House

A kid walks into the ice cream parlor.

"Chocolate peanut butter chip please!"

She takes the double scoop in her tiny hands and licks it, pushing the ice cream clean off the sugar cone with her tongue.

She is so shocked to see it plop on the floor that she just stands there, eyes wide.

Before she has a chance to react, the guy working there quickly serves another, presses it firmly into the cone, runs around the counter and places it into her hand.

"Here you go" he says. *"On the house."*

I was sitting there watching and thought it was so lovely and generous, what the guy did. It was not his fault the little girl dropped her ice cream.

But, can you imagine refusing to replace it? Why would you deeply disappoint a customer for so little?

This way, I will remember his kindness forever.

A Metaphor for Change

A guy is sitting next to me at a coffee shop and he's talking on the phone.

"No. No honey, it's easy. No — don't overthink it. I know, I know. We have a lot going on but you can totally do this. Yes. Yes you can. Just keep it simple. Start with a deep breath. It's not about what I do — it's about what you do. Yep. Yep. Yeah, I just add peanut butter."

Breakfast. A metaphor for change.

The Best Revenge

There is a famous elevator scene in the TV show Mad Men.

A guy is angry at Don Draper and with as much scorn as he can muster says to him *"I feel bad for you."*

To which Don Draper replies, *"I don't think about you at all."*

Breaking Me

I am at the airport standing a few feet from a guy who's having one of those fights that take everything out of you.

He's leaning against the wall, shaking with rage, yelling into the phone.

"I DON'T UNDERSTAND WHY DON'T YOU TRUST ME THIS IS SO HURTFUL!"

"NO NO JUST — NO!"

He is sobbing.

"THIS CAN'T KEEP HAPPENING I CAN'T DO THIS ANYMORE YOU ARE BREAKING ME!"

"LOOK LIKE I SAID I AM IN CHICAGO THE PLANE IS ABOUT TO TAKE OFF — NO NO STOP I CAN'T DO THIS NOW WE WILL TALK TONIGHT!"

He looks so terribly distraught my heart would go out to him.

Except, he is not in Chicago. He is in Newark.

Dependable

A couple gets in the elevator I am in.

He turns to her and says *"You know what, Rebecca? You feel about a Honda the way I feel about a Malbec. It's not going to blow me away but it's totally dependable."*

Double Negative

A few nights ago a friend and I went to an Indian restaurant.

There was an Indian couple sitting at the table next to ours.

"Mmm! This is good" she says to him. *"It's not not spicy."*

I think a double negative can be pretty perfect.

Finite Life Span

I'm in the office, and two people are talking in the kitchen about a hanging plant.

Her: *I don't know. I just don't know. Am I watering it too much? Am I not watering it enough?*

Him: *Yeah. It's so hard to tell.*

Her: *I don't know what to do. I just really don't want to kill it.*

Him: *Well, sometimes they just die, you know.*

Her: *WHAT?*

Him: *Yeah, they have a finite life span. It runs its course.*

Her: *WHAT, NO!*

It turns out hanging plants teach me everything I struggle to learn about relationships.

The Dog

A man gets on the bus with his dog on a short leash.

A woman on the other side of the bus screams.

"Keep that dog away from me!"

"Thank you for letting me know you don't like dogs," the man says. *"We will get out on the next stop."*

He sat there, gently holding his dog close to him as we waited for the bus door to open.

Loving, Sweet Thing

I'm sitting outside at a coffee shop in Singapore. A woman across from me is talking to someone but is alone. She's saying such loving, sweet things.

"You, yes, you. I love you. You are so beautiful. You are. You are the best. You have my heart."

I look at her ears assuming she must be on the phone — nothing.

It takes me a full five minutes to figure out she's talking to a curly haired puppy nestled in her purse.

Energy Drink

A guy in my Uber pool is complaining about being tired.

Him: *I don't understand. I pound energy drinks!*

Me: *Have you tried sleep?*

Him: —

Sigh.

Habit Forming

I have always experienced trouble sleeping and a friend was trying to persuade me to take sleeping pills.

"I'd rather not," I said. *"If at all possible I prefer not to depend on medication."*

"I know these are not habit forming," she said to me. *"Trust me. I would know. I have been taking them for 20 years."*

Hmph

Me: I had a really interesting day! In the morning I walked towards yoga and it was surprisingly warm. Then, the class was unexpected — the teacher I typically go to had a sub who was really terrific. I need to find out where else she teaches because I'd really like to take her class again. After that I came home and showered and spent some time writing. It was hard, actually. It was not what I would call an easy writing day. Then I went to a gig: a client wanted my help assembling a crisis plan, so I worked with multiple teams who would have to work together should an issue arise. After that I met a friend for appetizers and we caught up. It's funny how quickly time goes by, how you hold friends so dear and then months pass without you ever catching up in person. I mean, where does the time go? What about you? How was your day?

Him: Hmph. Good.

Old

I am walking down the street and a young woman is washing her car. She is wearing an AC/DC t-shirt.

"Hey! I like your t-shirt!" I say.

"Oh," she says. *"It's my grandma's."*

And how is your week going?

Zapata

A guy walks up to me at an event and reads my name badge out loud.

"Dushka Zapata. Is that really your name?"

"Yes," I say.

"Wow. Wow! Great name, great name! Tell me. Do you know who Zapata was? You know, Emiliano Zapata?"

"Yes."

"He was a hero of the Mexican revolution. Land and liberty is what he stood for. And, do you know what 'Dushka' means?"

"Yes".

"It's Russian. It means 'my little soul.'"

Thank you, kind sir, for thrice overriding my "yes" and explaining my own name to me.

Vexation

"You're always leaving," my friend says.

"Or," I say, *"I'm always visiting."*

Your life cannot be that bad if the most frequent vexation you deal with is that the people you love want more of you.

Safety Pin

This morning, as I was getting dressed, I noticed that a button on my dress was popping open, revealing, ummm, too much cleavage.

As I ran around getting ready to leave my house I forgot about it.

I arrived at the office and ran upstairs. As soon as I got to my desk my very good friend and coworker glanced over at me and reached into her purse.

"Here, sweetheart," she said, handing me a safety pin. *"I'll trade you a pin for a cup size."*

Matchbox

I was around 17 years old, at a party with a group of friends. It was noisy. People were drinking. Things were getting out of hand. I wanted to go home.

A guy, one of my closest, dearest friends, was very drunk. He walked over to me and was slurring something I couldn't understand.

"What?" I say. *"Honestly, I have no idea what you're saying."*

"I love you," he shouts over the music. He hangs his head down. *"I love you."*

"Let's get out of here," he adds. *"Let's just leave. I can take you home, and we can talk."*

"You are too drunk to drive," I say. *"Give me your car keys."*

We get into a disjointed argument I can't seem to connect, where he is explaining his feelings and I'm trying to take away his car keys. He gets into the car. He opens the door.

"This is it, Dushka," he says. *"This is us. This is our chance. Get in the car."*

I am in despair. I am asking him not to drive. I am telling him not to get in the car. *"Are you getting in the car?"* he says. *"Are you, or not?"*

He interprets the scene I am making as a personal rejection. He gets angry. He jumps into the car and drives off.

I run back into the party and find another friend. I explain what happened — not the love part but the *"he was very drunk and just drove off"* part. We both leap into the car to try to go find him.

I witness from the seat of one car the accident of the other. It looks unreal, small, light, like a matchbox. It swerves around, loses control, flips over. Flips over again.

We call an ambulance. The police arrive. One of them says to the other — *"Look at the car. Look at the roof, how it crumpled. If that kid had had anyone in the passenger seat, he'd be looking at involuntary manslaughter."*

How I See

I'm crouching over a plant taking a picture of it. A woman walks by and stops.

"Hey," she says. *"Is that a special kind of plant?"*

"I don't know," I say. *"I just think it's pretty."*

"So, you walk around taking pictures of plants?"

"Yep," I say. *"I sure do."*

"Can I see the picture?"

I show it to her.

"Wow," she says. *"I'd never seen that plant look quite like that. What else do you do?"*

"I'm a writer."

"Oh. So, you show people the way you see things, not just the way they are."

"Yes," I say. *"That's what I do."*

In the Way

I sometimes dog-sit for a dog named Lucy.

Lucy is incredibly expressive. If I pay attention, I understand pretty much everything she is trying to tell me.

For example, Lucy has two brushes — one is like a rake, for her undercoat, the other is really soft, for places like her ears, her face, her belly. The first time I took the rake in my hands she looked at me and tucked in her tail. *"I won't ever use it on your tail,"* I said.

Another example: when we get home, she likes it when I fill her water bowl and set it down. If we walk into my place and I start doing other things, she has this look. *"Hey,"* she says. *"Don't forget my water bowl."*

We say a lot, without words. *Do you want to come over here so I can give you scritchies? Oh yeah right there that's the spot. Hey I have to do some work so I have to look at my computer for a while. Excuse me, can we go outside now?*

There are many important words that she completely understands. Yes. No. (And, requests like sit, down, stay.)

And, there are a few things I wish I could impress upon her. When my friend drops her off she feels quite anxious. She whimpers. *"He's coming back,"* I say.

I want her to understand me when I say *"I will do my best to keep you safe. I will see that you have everything you need."*

I want her to know I love her. I want her to understand me when I say *"thank you for sometimes coming to stay with me."*

Water. Yes. No. Love. Safe. Thank you. I adore words. They are my joy, and also my livelihood. But maybe we don't need them as much as we think we do. Maybe sometimes they just get in the way.

A Few Days Off

One day, my then husband and I were driving home from work talking about how tired we were.

"Let's take a few days off and go to Puerto Vallarta" I said. *"We'd only have to pay for the plane tickets. We can stay at a friend's place."*

We go home and get online to book the tickets. He says *"the best price is on Alaska Airlines."*

As he tells me he's found the right deal at the right time on the days we want, he suddenly stops and looks at me and frowns.

"Yeah," I say. *"Let's keep it simple and drive somewhere instead."*

Like we both completely lost interest at the exact same time.

The flight we were planning to be on crashed. There were no survivors.

Rescuer

Sometimes Boyfriend and I are at some social function and someone walks up to me and says *"Dushka, hello! It's so great to see you! What are you doing here?"*

I have a lot of trouble recognizing people when I see them outside the context I usually interact with them in, so I stand there in a state of utter panic.

Boyfriend instantly, smoothly steps forward, ever so subtly shielding me with his body. He holds out his hand. *"Hello!"* he says. *"I'm Dushka's boyfriend."*

So the person shakes Boyfriend's hand and says *"I'm Andrea! It's so nice to finally meet you!"*

And that's how he rescues me.

Serenade

I board a flight from Mexico City to San Francisco and find my seat. There is a woman sitting next to me. As the plane takes off she looks out the window and cries.

I fully open the blind for her.

"Thank you," she sobs.

Her: *"Have you ever been in a relationship with a Mexican man?"*

Me: *"Yep."*

Her: *"I've never experienced anything like it. I mean, how do you get over someone who serenades you?"*

"Honey," I say. *"Fasten your seatbelt."*

Magnolias and Lockdowns

"Hey," I say to the man gardening his front yard, *"is this your tree?"*

He stares at me.

"Magnolias are my favorite," I say. *"I wanted to tell you that your tree makes me happy."*

He stares at me.

"Most magnolia trees bloom once a year," I say. *"And yours blooms way more often than that. It's magnificent."*

"It's been three weeks since I last spoke to anyone," he says. *"I'm sorry. It took my brain a moment to remember how."*

"Oh," I say. *"Well, I have time."*

I take a step away to show I am not implying breaking our required distance. He does the same. We sit and talk from afar for about 30 minutes, about plants, about the rain, about the proper care of a tree that insists on blooming more than it's supposed to.

"I'm glad my tree made a difference for you," he says. *"Because you just did the same for me."*

109

I've Given Up on That

We're sitting at the counter of a brand new restaurant near our house. We wonder how to order. Here, or at the cash register?

"Order at the cash register," says the guy sitting next to us. *"They'll give you digits."*

I feel a sense of total delight that he said "digits" rather than "a number". *"Digits!"* I say, only louder.

They bring our counter-neighbors their food. One ordered an open face tomato sandwich. The other a porky cheesy concoction with a poached egg perched gently on top.

I stare.

"You want to see me cut into this egg, don't you?"

He generously pushes the plate towards me and removes all the things obstructing my view. A glass. A cup. The salt shaker.

I feel I have the best seat in the house.

He deftly slips a knife over the top of the egg. The yolk oozes over everything masterfully, uniformly.

"Oooooh." I say. Out loud. I clap.

Playing it cool. I've gladly given up on ever learning how to play it cool.

Time Is Relative

One morning I got up early to write. My then boyfriend came downstairs at around 8:30 and asked if I wanted breakfast.

"Let me write for a little longer," I said. *"Then we can have breakfast together."*

A bit later he came back.

"You must be starving. Do you want anything?"

"Not really," I said. *"I meant what I just told you. Give me a little time and we can have breakfast together."*

"Breakfast?" he says. *"Dushka, it's 5:00 in the afternoon."*

Witness

My friend Jim was in a frightening car accident and posted about the experience on Facebook. *"If you are ever a witness, stop,"* he said. *"For police reports and insurance purposes, reporting what you saw can really help a person in distress."*

The very next day Boyfriend and I witnessed an accident. A car swerved into another lane and despite her efforts to get out of the way, despite driving off the road, the vehicle hit her and totaled her car.

"Do you want to get out?" Boyfriend said as he pulled over. *"Do you want to be a witness?"*

"We have to!" I said. *"Jim just told us how important it was!"*

So we stopped. The woman who swerved off the road was so upset. She was crying and shaking. *"He drove right into me! I tried to get out of his way!"*

I hugged her and held her and patted her back. *"We saw everything,"* I said. *"You have nothing to worry about. This was not your fault."* Then, I told her about our friend and how he had just told us the previous day that we needed to stop.

Later that evening we called Jim, who met us for dinner. *"Your instructions really helped someone tonight,"* we said as we told him what had happened.

If you learn about something someone can do to help another, spell it out. Put it out there. Before that accident ever took place, Jim had already sent us out to the rescue.

Crack

It was Sunday and the sky was cloudless and a group of friends and I spent the day at an amusement park. It was really fun and after a day of riding roller coasters and driving bumper cars my buddy offered to give me a ride home.

I lived close by and was feeling giddy and never considered the day could possibly end the way it did.

We left the amusement park at twilight. It was neither full day nor completely night: the kind of liminal light that affects visibility. Driving towards my house my friend took a wrong turn.

We ended up driving down a narrow alley, and I saw a pile of cement — from a construction site — right in the middle of the road.

It was kind of nonsensical for it to be there which is why it took my brain a second to put together what was about to happen. My friend didn't see it and without reducing her speed drove the car straight into it. It was like hitting a wall.

The next instant was all sound. Slamming, crunching, screeching, scraping, grinding.

Except, before all that, I heard a sound she didn't hear.

A loud, clean crack.

I had never heard such a sound and yet I knew what it was.

"Oh no," she said after a moment. *"Are you ok?"*

"My arm is broken," I said.

"Well, maybe it's just bruised."

"No," I said. *"It's broken."*

"How can you be so sure?"

"Because," I said. *"I heard it."*

Pandemic Compliment

I am walking around. A guy walks in my direction and waves. I wave back. It's so awkward and strange, so I say:

"I am smiling at you from under my face mask."

"Oh. You may not be aware of this," he says. *"But you are smiling at me with your entire energy field."*

Anesthesia

The last time I was going to get general anesthesia, I told the anesthesiologist how deeply concerned I was with how it would feel.

"I understand your concern," he said. *"Do me a favor and count to ten."* He gently fitted a mask over my face as I counted.

I felt relaxed.

Ah. How...nice.

"Anyway," I continued. *"It's kind of scary, this notion that you are going to put me to sleep and what if I wake up right in the middle of everything and feel suffocated or like I am trying to say something and you cannot hear me?"*

"I can assure you with 100% certainty that's not going to happen," he said.

"Ok, but how can you be so sure?"

"Because, Ms. Zapata. Your procedure is already over."

Electrified

I am in New York, walking towards a meeting with my friend and coworker Doug.

Me: *Wow. This city is electrifying.*

Him: *Dushka. You would be electrified in Boise, Idaho.*

Spring Chicken

A friend gives me a huge bear hug and a snuggle.

"I'm going to crack your back," he says. *"It will feel great — you've probably been sitting at your computer."*

Me: *"Yaaaas please."*

He hugs me and lifts me and squeezes me. He's deft. He's skilled. No cracking. None.

"My God, Dushka." He says. *"You have the spine of a spring chicken."*

18 Minutes

When I landed in Munich, I told someone from Lufthansa that I was a bit worried about making my connection to Berlin.

He looked at me like I was a small child.

Then, *"You will be at the gate of the next flight in 18 minutes, and you have an hour."*

"Ya," I said. *"But, I have to go through customs!"*

I was at the gate 18 minutes later.

Morning Person

A friend reaches out via WhatsApp early this morning.

Hey Dushka! You up? I'm in your neighborhood and super hungry. Join me for breakfast!

Me: *What are you doing in my neighborhood so early?*

Him: *It's too long and complicated to explain.*

Me: *You met a woman, went back to her place, and are sneaking out early.*

Him: *Damn. Uh, yep.*

I love that I'm a morning person. If I wasn't I'd sleep through so many interesting things.

Guardian Angel

It was early in the morning and I was walking across The Tenderloin (a pretty gritty San Francisco neighborhood) on my way to work.

A man who was standing across the street saw me and sprinted towards me, attempting to throw a blanket over my head. He seemed delirious.

At first I loudly told him to stand back, then tried to stride away. He stepped up his pace. I turned around and raced maybe half a block, saw an active construction site, and ducked inside.

"A man is chasing me," I said as I made my way in.

A construction worker instantly — faster than instantly — pushed me behind him and stepped between me and the door I had run in from. He was physically shielding me from the entrance.

The man who had been chasing me tried to get past him but the construction worker said, *"You need to leave"*. He shuffled away.

I caught my breath. *"Thank you so very much,"* I said.

"You have a good day, ma'am," he said.

I felt deeply grateful for his chivalry but it wasn't until later that it occurred to me the construction worker was outrageously brave. He had no idea who he was protecting me from — someone armed with a gun or a knife? Someone truly dangerous?

I think about him sometimes, how quickly he stepped in without giving the situation much consideration.

I think he was a hero, or a guardian angel with a hard hat.

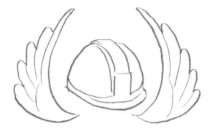

Greener Grass

I am sitting at a corner table in a restaurant and a woman walks in.

She catches my eye because her hair comes down to her arse. It's long and straight and shiny. It reminds me of a curtain. Her hair blocks the light. That's how thick it is.

My hair is wild and curly. Despite my yearning, my longing, I've never had it very long because it's a lot. But also because it doesn't really grow down.

I discreetly stare at this woman. I watch as she tilts her head to the side and gathers all her hair to swing it out of the way so she doesn't sit on it.

So she doesn't sit on it.

I finish my meal and get up and walk by her table to leave the restaurant.

"Oh my god," she says, looking at me. *"Oh my god. Look at your hair! My hair does nothing! Nothing! No matter what I do I can't even set it into a gentle wave. Tell me. What do you do? What do you do to it?"*

Me, eloquently: *"Umm nothing."*

Her: *"May I touch it?"*

I nod and move closer.

Her: *"My god. My god! I thought it would be coarse. It's soft! It's silky! You don't understand! You don't understand. I've dreamed all my life of having hair just like yours."*

Phobia

I have never broken the law in my life and yet have an irrational immigration officer phobia.

The night before I flew into Sri Lanka I tossed around. Would it be hard to get in? Would my visa be problematic?

The immigration officer asked the purpose of my visit. *"I am a tourist,"* I said. *"Sri Lanka is my vacation."*

She BEAMED. She lifted the stamp over my passport and as she brought it down she smiled at me.

"Thank you," she said. *"Thank you for choosing Sri Lanka."*

Uber Ride

I have been writing all morning and realize I need a break. I decide it's a good time to go run some errands.

I get in an Uber.

Him: *You Dushka?*

Me: *Yep.*

Him: *I am glad you're not the Dushka I know.*

Me: *I sure am too.*

Him: *It's what I used to call my ex-wife.*

Me: *Uh huh.*

Him: *She was terrible. Ugh.*

Me: *I am sorry.*

Him: *We sacrifice everything for the ones we love. Everything.*

Honestly. Stories follow me everywhere.

Profoundly Happy

I am having breakfast and a guy comes over and asks if he can sit with me.

He tells me he's from Sweden and has been coming to Sri Lanka for 20 years.

"Do you know why I wanted to sit with you?" He says. *"Because people who come here from far away are always seeking something, and you instead look profoundly happy."*

"Truer words," I responded, *"have never been spoken."*

Strangers and Connection

I was sitting alone at the counter at a restaurant and he walked up and sat next to me. He was with a friend.

The waiter set before me an order of deviled eggs and I noticed he was looking at them. *"They look great, don't they?"*

"They sure do," he said. *"What's that thing placed at the top?"*

"I don't know. Why don't you try one and tell me?"

I think he thought I was kidding. *"I can't eat your dinner,"* he said. *"Sure you can,"* I said. *"Honestly, I'm happy to share."*

First we talked about the ingredients in the deviled eggs. (He correctly guessed the delicate brown bits on top were fried onions, which I really appreciated because I was having trouble placing the flavor.)

Then we talked about what we did for a living and why we both happened to be sitting at that counter on the same day at the same time (he and his friend had gone somewhere else but it was too crowded, so they left and ended up here).

We spoke about the difference between flirting (fun, harmless, devoid of a goal or intent) and hitting on someone (intentional, directed). We agreed we were flirting.

We told each other how old we were (we both assumed the other was much younger — it turned out we were the same age).

Towards the end of the conversation we talked about relationships and told each other things about ourselves that were quite intimate. *"Wow,"* he said. *"What I just told you is not exactly a secret, but I don't think I've ever told anyone."*

"Why do you think you told me?"

"Because," he said. *"Strangers are not tangled up in your life. Sometimes it's easier to talk to someone you don't know than to someone you've known for years."*

Strangers, and a really good connection. Two of my favorite things.

Dazed

I am sitting at the back of the bus and a young woman sits next to me.

She looks dazed. She's dressed all in black and her top is black lace.

"Do you know how far we are from 16th Street?" she asks.

"Yeah," I say. *"About 4 stops. I can tell you when we get there."*

"I am all alone," she says. *"All alone. I will be alright."*

"Of course you will," I say.

She looks at me. Her eyes look dark and wild. *"My husband died,"* she says. *"Two days ago."*

I place my hand on top of hers and circle it with my fingers. I give her hand a squeeze.

"I will be alright," she says.

"Of course you will," I say. *"Of course you will."*

Like Babies

A woman sitting next to me at a restaurant sets her arm on the table, exposing a beautiful seaweed tattoo.

I ask her about it and she in turn asks if I have one.

"I don't," I say. *"I love them on other people but worry that if I get something I will get tired of it".*

"Nah," she says. *"Tattoos are like babies. If they are yours you love them even when you don't like them very much."*

Leniency

"I'm sorry I snapped at you," I tell Boyfriend.

"Don't mention it," he says. *"You have been under a lot of stress. I don't like it when you snap at me, but I understand it has nothing to do with me."*

My favorite acts of kindness are about a generosity of spirit, a leniency, towards the imperfections of others.

Object

Sometimes people write bad things about me online.

I show them to my friend and we roll our eyes.

He asks if they hurt my feelings. Most of the time I don't feel hurt, but I do feel perplexed.

Why attack a human being you don't even know?

"You are not a human being," he says. *"You are an object."*

I look at him.

"You are a human to me, and to the many people who know you, see you, love you. But, to people on an internet site you are an object. An abstract concept. That's what happens online. You are dehumanized."

So here is my wish to anyone who forgets everyone writing online is a person: I hope someone in your life knows you. I hope someone sees you. I hope you are loved.

Something Sexy

One Day

What time is it in the universe? Does anyone else out there feel like she is always running late? Is she surrounded by darkness?

Am I looking up now or millions of years ago? Or a million years from now?

What is it that gives a galaxy its colossal, swirling shape? Who is the cosmic sculptor?

Are light and energy the same thing? Is it cold out there? Is there heat? Do stars turn on and off?

What is dark matter, exactly? And how many of the things out there also exist inside of me? Does my blood contain glittering, swirling, galactic formations?

One day I will find a warm, remote location devoid of light pollution. I will lay out a soft blanket and lie beside someone who can answer all these questions.

He will point out constellations across the sky and locate the identical match to the light sprinkling of beauty marks that span the width of my shoulders.

How Was Your Morning?

My building is normally quiet but this morning someone is having very loud sex.

She's screaming, dogs start howling, and someone goes to someone else's apartment to bang on the door and yell.

There's a back story here full of intrigue and, well.

I'm happy to report that my life has gotten to the point where I don't even need to leave my bed to come across something juicy to write about.

Casual Sex

Some people have casual sex, no strings attached, consider it loads of fun, and cavort off into the sunset.

Other people are particularly sensitive to whatever hormones are released during sex, get emotionally entangled, stare adoringly at the person they just had sex with and blurt out that they love them.

I belong in the second category and as such recognize that I am incapable of having sex while remaining emotionally uninvolved.

Urgency

Almost every movie has a scene like this.

A couple, kissing under the doorframe. He fumbles with the keys. They trip inside, grope as they push against the entrance wall.

They jostle around. He spots the dining room table. It is covered in piles of stuff.

He releases her, turns around, leans both his forearms on the table and sweeps everything to the floor, everything, then sets her down on the now cleared, spacious surface.

Writing carries this same urgency.

Excuse me — I have to go. Just let me go. My brain has been trying to articulate this thought, and is starting to organize it. I just need to put it down, to pin it, fast. I don't want to lose it. If I do, it will be gone forever.

I look for a space, a surface, privacy, silence, shush, go away, everyone go away, and spot a table covered in stuff and lean my forearms down and sweep it clean.

I pull out a notebook or a napkin or a crayon or my computer and sit down and oh my god finally. I write.

Sex Outside

It was the middle of the night and I was at Burning Man, trudging along the Deep Playa.

A couple had set a blanket down and was having sex out there in the fringes of a dry lake bed.

They had surrounded themselves with blinking lights, because out there if you are not visible you can get run over by an art car.

The moment I happened upon was not open, not an act of exposure or exhibitionism. It was intimate. There they were, his hands around her hip bones, her dusty back arched, covered in butterfly tattoos.

I wanted to turn away and give them a bit of privacy but for a beat I stopped and looked because it was beautiful.

Women

I often find myself ogling women that I find beautiful; their strength and their radiance (or their shoes).

I often feel enchanted by their company and the sense of kinship and camaraderie that is so very different from the kinship and camaraderie I get from the presence of a man.

I often feel lit up by a woman.

But when I think about sex with a woman, a switch flips off. Nothing is left. Not even curiosity.

So yes, I feel attracted. Very attracted. But alas, not like that.

Bounty

I just got home from a week in Chicago for work and am sitting at the bar in a restaurant close to where I live having a bite because my fridge is empty.

I thought I was done writing for the day, but that's when a couple comes over, sits next to me and begins to discuss their sexual fantasies.

They are describing the orgy of their dreams, what they like and don't like about their bodies and how she wishes she could be a gay man for a day.

Honestly. I don't know what I've done to deserve such a bounty.

Things I've Kissed

I've kissed goodbye something that was once important.

I've kissed and made up, so I've also kissed reconciliation.

I've kissed envelopes to seal them. A kiss is embossment, an engraving, an insignia, a secret. I don't kiss and tell.

I've kissed air, fog, pollution, mist, sunshine and rain when I've blown someone a kiss from across the street.

I've tried things that have not worked out so I guess my work — an extension of me — has often kissed the dust.

Once, during a particularly long, harrowing drive, I said *"if we make it to our destination alive, I will kiss the ground I walk on"* and we did, so I did.

I've kissed necks and lips and other warm, memorable places but I will leave that out as people don't count as things.

Breathe Deeply

I had just begun regularly attending yoga classes.

He laid out his mat next to mine and a few minutes in I felt our flow from one pose to the other was connected. The class felt like our dance, balanced, cadenced, compatible.

In the last pose, Savasana, we lay there, side by side on our backs, eyes closed. I extended my arms out in a stretch and accidentally grazed his fingers with the back of my hand. He surprised me by moving his hand up against mine. We weren't holding hands as much as barely touching, two strangers who had never turned to squarely look at each other, never spoken.

As I sat up, bowed to the teacher and collected my props I thought about how little I wanted to talk to him, about how that 90 minute class was to me a complete love story, communicative, rhythmical, synchronized, in tune.

I folded my blanket and put the blocks in their place and reluctantly looked up. He was gone.

I wonder sometimes if he still attends yoga classes, what his story is, if he has found someone to breathe deeply with in a darkened room.

Eyes in the Back of Her Head

My boyfriend and I were madly making out and heard my mom had come home earlier than expected.

I threw my shirt back on and went upstairs to nonchalantly say hello.

It would be a breeze. My recent activity would fly under the radar, undetected.

What kills me is she didn't even turn around.

Me: *Hi mom!*

Her: *Hi honey. Your shirt's on backwards.*

It's a Date

If I invite a guy over to my house and we sit on the couch facing each other, the soles of my feet against his, and we read, that's a date.

Giving each other hand massages — or anywhere massages — is a date.

A grand tour of every high rise and hill in the city so we amass at least a dozen breathtaking views is a date.

Sitting on a park bench, strolling down Main Street, cycling up a back road, laying on the grass face up, side by side, watching the clouds go by.

Eating with our fingers, skipping a meal, flying to Paris, checking out houses we would like to buy but never could.

Me helping you clean out your closet, which might require that you model some outfits for me.

You helping me shop for a gala I need to attend, which might require that I model some outfits for you.

Me reading you a story — the one I wrote about you.

Soaking in a hot tub, an evening wandering around a museum, an evening co-creating an abstract painting, an evening without uttering a word.

Asking and answering questions, looking at old photo albums (look, that was me in high school), truth or dare, tea over Skype, you somewhere in South East Asia, me in San Francisco.

All these things could or could not be a date. We get to decide.

Things Lovers Discuss

"Hey, lover boy. Is all your laundry in the hamper? Whatever isn't will not get washed."

"Yo, boo. Can you please send me your supermarket list? I'm going to swing by after work."

"Oh, sugar — do we have plans for Saturday? A friend invited me for dinner but I can't remember if we already had something on the calendar."

Pick-up Artist

We had been dating for some time but were not yet living together. We were having dinner at a restaurant and debating if we wanted dessert.

Suddenly, he dipped his index finger in his glass of water and flicked the water at me, lightly sprinkling me. Then he winked.

"Come on, sweetheart," he says to me, *"Let's get you home and out of those wet clothes."*

What I Fantasize About

Sex, by far.

Except, not sex.

I fantasize about details before I fantasize about going all the way.

I am talking to someone and *wow wait a minute I think I like you* and before I even consider taking off his clothes (in my imagination) I wonder what it would be like to lean over and nuzzle the side of his neck.

I mean, he's so close.

I wonder what he smells like.

What it would be like to put my mouth up against the rim of his ear.

For his reaction, but mostly for me.

Sex with each person is completely different so I wonder what he likes. I linger there, on all this wondering.

I don't think of a bed or rumpled sheets or a hotel room — come on, it's too soon to go anywhere near there — but please. Find me a nook where time can stand still so I can trace with my fingers the life line that runs across the palm of his hand.

Can we shut the world out, you and I? If so I would maybe trace the life lines that run across the soles of his feet.

Hands. Feet. Which one, I wonder, would allow me to more accurately read his future?

It's not that the part of my brain that fantasizes isn't extravagant or elaborate.

It's not that she is prone to any kind of sublimation.

It's that she believes discovery and anticipation are vastly underrated.

Something Loving

Love Stories

Love stories are everywhere. They fall softly around us, light, translucent, designed to provide an effervescent counterpoint, a deliverance, to our inherent sense of unsettlement, entrapment and despair.

They are gossamer, delicate and clear. They are salvation.

We pile crap all over them.

We demand immediate clarity. Definition, from something nascent. We clamor for answers but the answers don't yet exist.

What does this mean? Where is this going?

We throw on top of that unbearably heavy things: I want. I demand. I expect. Then, the heaviest burden of all.

Forever.

Most love stories are simple, sheer, resplendent connections. They are a thin, breathless layer of nothing. They are hopeless, not because they lack hope but because they've had no time. Secret, not because they are wrong but because they are fragile.

They feel like light, like a free fall, and have no outlook. It's not a lack of future. It's that they exist outside of our inane chronology.

The best love stories have no meaning. They are irrational, unanalytical, fearless and kinetic. They keep you up at night with incessant daydreaming. You have no choice but to resort to fantasy.

They remind you to break free, imagine, remember.

It's this. This is what I used to want, back before things got so fucking complicated.

You contemplate escaping to a fragrant country and taking up praying after a lifetime without a God.

Please wait right here. Let these stories take a breath or two before you burden them with meaning. Don't define them. Don't even articulate them.

Let them never be.

Magic Red Beans

When I was growing up in Mexico City, adults would go to restaurants and have lunches that would go on forever.

Long after three or four course meals were consumed, they would sit at the *"sobremesa"* and have long, torturous, never ending conversations about mind numbing things.

Fortunately for us, some of these restaurants they frequented had enormous grassy gardens with big trees that bore magic red beans.

When adults got tired of our bouncing, our restlessness and our whining (please can we go now? What about now?) they would say: *"go out into the garden and pick as many magic red beans as you can. Then bring them to us. When we deem them to be enough, we can go."*

My mom still has leftover loot in a bowl on her living room floor.

163

Bench

I was sitting on a bench during recess.

A boy came over with two bags of potato chips.

He sat next to me and handed me one of the bags.

"Hey, thank you!" I said. *"Is this a date?"*

"Yup," he said.

Primal Puzzle

It was recess and my friends and I were sitting on a bench snacking, gabbing.

A guy I had never seen before walked across the yard and I dropped whatever I was putting in my mouth.

I couldn't take my eyes off him.

"Who is that?"

"His name is Wallace," said my friend. *"He has been dating Monica's sister for some time."*

"Isn't. He. Stunning?"

My friends looked at me like I was nuts. *"I mean, he's OK."*

Wallace moved in a different circle and attended different classes and every time he crossed my line of vision I dropped things. I blushed. I stammered.

I don't know why certain things arrest us. The obvious answer is that it's because they are beautiful. To me it's more than that.

It feels like I am recognizing something of unspeakable value — the solution to a primal puzzle — that I didn't know I had lost, and that I long to recover.

What Makes Something 10 Times Better?

I had a friend whose mom was an amazing cook.

My friend's brother lived abroad and whenever he visited, my friend made it a point to invite me to his house for dinner.

"My mom's food is never better than when she's feeding my brother after not seeing him for months."

It's love, I think. It makes everything ten times better.

Ruin the Moment

Many years ago I met a guy at a beach resort in Mexico, where I am from.

We started talking at the pool, later walked over to the beach, strolled along the water, had a late lunch of tacos and guacamole and sat down on towels to watch the sun go down.

As the sky turned orange and purple and pink I could tell he was thinking about leaning over to kiss me.

I didn't want to kiss him — I liked him but not like that — but I really didn't want to ruin such a beautiful moment.

What to do?

It turns out I didn't have to think about it very much at all. As he came closer, my body recoiled on its own.

He was angry. As if kissing me was his right. *"I can't believe you would ruin a sunset,"* he said.

His response was so disagreeable and such a contrast to how pleasant he had been earlier that he made me feel proud of my reaction instead of regretful.

If I don't feel like doing something I won't do it no matter what I might be doing to the moment.

If I ruin a moment, I know I can create many other beautiful ones.

Three Precious Words

The person who loves me is my ally, my accomplice, a steady presence through life.

I want us to be there for each other — not necessarily to assist or support, but to *witness.*

Holidays, birthdays, weddings, milestones.

I made a new friend. I have a new job. I reached that goal I worked so hard for.

Look. Look at what is happening to my life.

Hey, I am afraid.

Let me share my thoughts with you. I have so much to say. Here. Take my words.

Tell me. Talk to me. Show me.

At a doctor's appointment, in the park on a Sunday afternoon, on a long, transcontinental flight, at a funeral, in the hospital, at a celebratory dinner, at a reunion.

"I am here."

Kathia

My brother's ex-wife is like a sister to me.

She and I were walking around LA and I suddenly saw the most beautiful, most perfect flower I had ever laid eyes on.

It stunned me so much that I teared up.

I turned to discreetly look at her to determine if she had seen me cry at a flower (oh, Dushka) and that's when I noticed she was crying too.

I remember that moment as so filled with beauty — at the flower that took my breath away but also at the blooming of pure love I felt towards someone who experienced this flower just like I did.

Beginnings

In the very beginning *oh my god I like him so much. I wonder if he likes me.* And I could ask him, but he doesn't have the answers I really want.

Are you who I think you are? Is this going to last?

He put his hand on my arm and I felt a jolt. Hello, chemistry. I furiously wondered what our first kiss would be like and then what sex would be like. And then sex was so awesome we'd forget to eat.

Don't get me wrong. I know the value of what's real. The value of day in, day out. The value of showing up. The value of a relationship that has stood up against a thousand inevitable disappointments. The value of your name being the name that springs to mind when I need an emergency contact. I know about the work we can do to keep things fresh.

But, still. Beginnings. Beginnings, all spark and splendor and hunger. That is what I would reclaim.

You Keep Coming Back

We were in that very early pre-relationship phase where you are getting to know each other and the relationship has not yet taken a specific shape.

I knew I really liked him and that whatever was going on felt like more than just a friendship.

He calls me and says *"I want us to be committed to each other,"* to which I reply *"can you tell me what you mean by that?"*

To which he instantly says *"commitment means you keep coming back."*

And that's what he does.

I'd Do That

The song I'm listening to is saying *"I'd step in front of a train for you".*

I've felt that way so many times. I'd take a bullet for you. I'd put my hand in the fire for you.

But, why? Why must my love destroy me? Why am I so quick and willing to obliterate myself?

Why can't it build me up?

I'll jump on a train for you. I will travel the world and fill my eyes with its splendor.

I will survive everything for you. I will thrive for you. I will write my name across the light blue, concave curve of the sky for you, sweep the clouds aside.

I will leave everywhere beautiful things intended to sprout, to bloom, to take hold in others.

This way, maybe my love — rather than finishing me off — might live forever.

Why Do You Love Me?

In my experience, when someone asks *"why do you love me?"* what he is really looking for is a verbal snuggle.

You know, a nuzzle, a cuddle, a caress, a fondle with words.

I love you because you shuffle when you walk.

Because different parts of you have different textures, like a feast, like a tactile buffet.

I love you because your view of the world is different from mine which means I get to see it my way and then I get to see it yours. Like discovering I have extra windows, a rooftop terrace with a view.

I love you because of your interest in things I can't fathom being interested in and because after a careful review of the menu you never fail to order the last thing I would choose.

I love you because you're good, a good person, and I feel lucky that you at any time could go anywhere and here you are, with me.

Cufflinks/Blue Jeans

I dated a guy once who dressed impeccably. I loved his just shined shoes and large watches and the short, tapered hair on the back of his neck. I decided then and there I had a thing for flawlessly dressed men.

I dated another guy who didn't even notice if his socks matched. He was lanky and untidy and disheveled and beautiful. He had a few well worn flannel shirts he didn't mind lending me and did not even own a belt. I decided I had a weakness for long haired, scruffy guys.

It turns out that what I like is individuals and their peculiarities. One for how deftly he managed to make a perfect knot in his tie, the other for the uneven way he wore down his sneakers, the washed out color of his once blue jeans.

Registry

Once, eons ago, I was in that distant place in my life where I was planning my wedding.

One of the traditional things to do was create a registry: a list of gifts my then fiancé and I assembled so that guests would know what we needed for our new life.

Gripped by enthusiasm, we requested every possible kitchen gadget.

This is how I ended up with a fully souped up kitchen: we had a sandwich maker, a bread maker, a watermelon slicer, a pancake batter mixer, a waffle maker, a multi-function cooker, a blender that looked like a rocket ship, an elite countertop oven and so much more.

We used none of it.

Since that day we sat in our living room ripping open all the gifts we never used, I am divorced, live in a smaller place and don't cook at all.

Even as a person who doesn't ever cook, I own a top of the line Japanese knife that gives me a frisson of sheer joy when I slice anything; and a French coffee press my man uses to make me coffee every morning.

I am happier than I've ever been, which may or may not be related to all the space I have on my kitchen counter.

Love Language

I think we are all a quagmire, a tight morass of ego, insecurities, the scars of what we've been through, our body reacting in a way we don't fully own or understand, our emotions getting away from us, our judgment and tendency to interfere.

My love language is my own and another person's ability to see the me that exists beyond all that, the person I really was before I got tangled up in all this humanness.

Fate

Love makes me believe in fate.

I can't fathom how we met the way we did, so many years after the first time we quickly shook hands in that conference room. I can't fathom this happened the way it did. What are the chances? Remember how the whole world was on pause? Remember how we walked across a city engulfed in smoke?

I can't fathom it happened right when it did, the perfect intersection, the most fortuitous moment, not just for you but for both of us.

Watching anyone defy their circumstances makes me not believe in fate. It shows me we are powerful, architects of our destiny, audacious. Time and time again we bend the most obvious path into one that can only feel like the direct result of what we've done.

The notion that any universal power would even bother with the task of writing out our lives strikes me as implausible. I think all of it is in our courageous, often incompetent hands and that we are an unbearable mix of effort, fortune and accident.

FATE

Intersection

She likes her hand held when she walks, her elbow linked, an arm around her. It's the warmth, the contact, but mostly it's the tether. For a moment she feels like she belongs to someone, which is illusory because despite her best efforts she can never stop being free.

He travels with his passport and keeps in his wallet currencies of many countries. It's possibility, adventure, but mostly it's the freedom. He feels he belongs to no one, which is illusory because despite his best efforts the fact that he is a family man is immutable.

When their lives briefly intersect they recognize in the other what they have lost. And it's the clear, moonlit reflection of what we can never have that we can't help but regard as captivating.

Eyes

I've looked deep into someone's eyes and had the sensation that I could see everything.

Like an involuntary free fall into something still and deep and ever-changing, like wide open ocean water, where I could clearly make out sorrow and despair and hunger and desire and exhaustion and determination and loss.

Like it was all evident and clear and offered up to me.

Like I don't know how to thank you, how to honor what you have so very openly allowed me to see.

Honestly.

Every bit I saw was beautiful.

Lucy

This week, I looked after a beast. Her name is Lucy.

She bounds up the stairs and I feel like a feather. Like a kite.

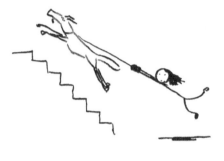

Lucy loves grass. Grass is a party.
Grass is elation. Grass is life.

A boy spots Lucy from afar.

"DOGGIE!" He dashes over.

I ask Lucy to sit. I ask the boy to be gentle.

He put his tiny arms around her big head. Lucy bows.

One evening, we were having dinner outside. Another dog rushed towards us.

Lucy growled.

Before bed, we snuggle.

At night she prowls around my apartment.

She settles down by the door.

I can't believe I get to love her.

Sexy and Light

On our first date we talked about how crushing it is to break up with someone you love.

"Yeah," he said. *"It makes you feel that you might be unlovable."*

I teared up.

As we sat there looking at each other I felt both exposed and grateful. Grateful that we skipped the small talk. Grateful that we were being real and capable of being susceptible.

I suppose it's weird to start out by being both intense and vulnerable right when everyone advises you to keep things "sexy and light" but it was the sense that I could see right into his heart that made me feel like I had to see him again.

Magic

I cry at weddings.

It's the bald-faced love, the earnestness, the holding out of your heart to another, so naked and open and true.

But it's also that we, bewildered by love, make promises we don't know we can keep.

Do we really completely govern our own heart?

I was at a wedding last night and overheard that the brother of the groom is a talented magician. I walked over to him and asked if the rumors were true. He pulled a pack of cards out of his suit pocket and asked me to inspect it.

He then fanned out the deck with such dexterity I felt my heart leap. He asked me to pick a card and I did and he reshuffled it into the deck as I stood there looking at the blur of his long fingers.

"I'm pretty sure it's not this one," he said, as he pulled out a card and flipped it over in front of me.

I shook my head no.

He took that very same card and rubbed it against his thigh.

"Now it is," he said. I clapped.

I love my friends so much. They are so young and the presence of the other has made them both better people. They exhibit the kind of love that very well could last forever.

Plus, magic runs in the family.

Coffee Maker

Boyfriend makes me coffee.

He owns an elaborate espresso machine, equivalent to 50 pounds of metal that sits on our kitchen counter and serves to pour two ounces of coffee.

He grinds the beans, froths almond milk, artfully pours the shot of espresso on top. Then, he hands it to me in my special cup.

He is very picky about the beans. I can never really tell the difference. I would drink whatever so I guess that would make me quite adventurous.

When we're not home he is the coffee purveyor. He researches the best coffee place he can find and we walk over before we've even had breakfast.

At Burning Man we had with us a bottle of cold brew concentrate that he mixed with ice and almond milk creamer. It was delicious.

For me, a "coffee maker" refers to a significant other, not a machine.

What Makes Love So Sweet?

Let me tell you about my favorite almond cookie.

It's dense and covered in powdered sugar.

The last time I had one I introduced a friend to it.

He bit into it, covering the corners of his mouth with a dusting of powdered sugar.

Then he slightly leaned forward and licked his fingers.

He nodded.

"This is a good cookie."

Full disclosure: I have a tendency to introduce people to this cookie. It's not exclusive.

I buy it, hand it over. We sit outside in the sun and savor it and go *mmmm.*

We comment on the crisp and crunch of the outside, the soft center.

It's always so nice.

Anyway, now when I eat this cookie, aside from almonds and sugar and eggs it is imprinted with the gentle papery memory of the people I've shared it with.

This makes it so much better.

This makes everything better.

That's what makes love sweet.

The Waiter

My friend Shana was at a restaurant having dinner with friends. Service was chaotic, disorganized. She noticed there was one waiter who seemed to be working three times as hard, taking charge, coordinating others, and picking up the slack.

She was mesmerized by his grit and how seriously he was taking his job. She couldn't take her eyes off him.

Before she left the restaurant that night she did something completely out of character.

She wrote out her phone number on a piece of paper and handed it to him on her way out.

Last night I attended their wedding.

What's the Best Vacation You've Ever Had?

We used to stop time.

We'd steal an afternoon and squander it in my apartment.

(Believe me when I tell you squandering time is the best thing you can do with it.)

We'd step inside and close the door and revel in that initial moment of awkwardness.

Then, step closer to each other.

He'd gently lean in to kiss me.

He had the most beautiful mouth.

Or I'd run my hand down the length of his back, so warm and so smooth.

I would look right into his eyes and he would look right into mine and what I felt was that I could see everything.

From the very first time it felt so much like love.

I felt like I loved him, even though at first I didn't, and it felt like he loved me.

Which maybe in a way he did.

My favorite part is that we created a space outside this world. It was not tangled in our life or our social dynamics, not related to work or family. There were no obligations, no demands, no strings. There were no entanglements.

I would say there were no expectations, except that would be a lie.

But, that came later.

Before that, it was so easy. I set aside my life, the things that weighed me down, the things that worried me or snarled me or snagged on me.

Before that, nothing existed during those afternoons — nothing but him and the startling feast he was to my senses.

It was him.

That's the best vacation I've ever had.

Chicken Sandwich

"Dushka," he said. *"I happen to be in your neighborhood and wonder if you'd like to have coffee with me."*

Oh heck yas.

"Heck yas! See you in a bit!"

We order coffee through a window protected by plexiglass. We can't sit — the sitting section in the coffee shop has been cordoned off — so he asks if I want to walk. (Yes, please.)

We wander around my neighborhood, then down and around the park, then up the hill.

It's very hot and very dry, and the backdrop of our walk is a series of plumes of black smoke — evidence of so many fires raging in the periphery of the city.

Everything smells like it's burning.

San Francisco is mostly deserted, and the few people we see wear masks, look dazed, walk fast, make no eye contact.

We can't seem to stop talking.

After a few hours we get hungry so find a take-out chicken sandwich and eat it facing each other on a bench outside.

I can't tell you how good that sandwich was, how crispy. It had some kind of tangy spicy sauce, and crunchy pickles. Might this be the best sandwich I've ever had?

"Gawd," he says. *"Is this the best sandwich you've ever had?"*

We end up spending most of the day together, and I wonder how something so marvelous can sprout out of nowhere in times that can only be described as apocalyptic.

Even as I spent time with him I wish I could spend more time with him. *"I wish I could spend more time with you,"* he says.

So this is what we do.

Luxury

I sometimes suffer from sleep paralysis. It's a frightening form of nightmare: I experience something that feels real in the limbo between being awake and being asleep, and can neither speak nor move.

Last night I woke up from a particularly unsettling episode and called my partner. I really needed to hear someone's voice to anchor me to reality, but also to keep me awake long enough to allow the dream world to recede rather than re-envelop me. I felt like I was resisting a riptide pulling me under.

I called someone at 4:00 am and he called me right back. He asked me to stay on the phone with him while he talked to me. Then he called again at 6:30 am to make sure I was OK.

Love is a luxury.

Kitchen Towels

The last time I lived with someone, ugh. I could never find a kitchen towel when I needed it.

Dushka! He'd say, exasperated. *Where the heck do the kitchen towels go?*

I'd roll my eyes, because look. I don't cook. I stay out of the kitchen. How was I supposed to know the fate of the kitchen towels?

Today, I live alone. And, ugh. I can never find a kitchen towel when I need it. Where the heck do they go?

So I pace around and find them all, scrunched up wherever I was last sitting.

Dirty Water Eyes

My man has dirty water eyes.

Aside from green, blue and gold flecked, they are also big and wide and so expressive. Sometimes when I look inside them I catch a glimpse of what I can only describe as absolute purity, as if he carried something in his soul that was still immaculate, untainted.

It's when I feel arrested by this sensation that I rub my nose on his and tell him he has dirty water eyes, swampy eyes or froggy eyes, depending on the light and the color of his sweater.

ROMANCE BY NUMBER:

1. OCEAN AZURE
2. FROGGY BLUE
3. SWAMPY GREEN
4. DIRTY WATER
5. FLECKS OF GOLD
6. DEEP POOL BLACK

Swiss Army Knife

My father always carried with him a Swiss Army Knife.

He reached into the pocket of his jeans to pull it out and open a wine bottle. To dig out a splinter from my index finger. To save me from picking on a hangnail. To cut a loose string from the hem of my sweater (with those tiny little scissors). To slice cheese or salami. To trim the frayed, unruly tips of my shoelaces.

After he died my brother found that Swiss Army Knife in the drawer by his bed. He grabbed it, handed it to me. *"Here,"* he said. *"I think you should take this."*

I have that Swiss Army Knife right by my desk. I never use it.

Why don't I let go of it?

Because. It's not the Swiss Army Knife I am holding onto.

What Are the Worst Travel Days of the Year?

I would say around Thanksgiving and around Christmas.

Every year right around now I run to the airport and look around and wonder what on earth compels us all to hop on a plane during the worst possible time to travel.

And then I remember.

It's love.

Other Things To Sip

It Never Gets Old

The first time I saw the Golden Gate Bridge I couldn't believe it. I had seen so many photographs, of course. But nothing could prepare me for this.

How could something be so stately, so defiant? How could it be so dainty? So pretty? How could it stand guard like that, so proud?

I moved to San Francisco many, many years later and visited her again. I walked from The Marina to Crissy Field, a long stretch of flat land along the water where you never lose sight of the Bridge. I couldn't get over her dignity. She manages to be imposing without being pompous or pretentious. I think it's the graceful proportions — grand, without ever being haughty.

I have been living in San Francisco for over twenty years and see her almost every day. Every time she makes me feel all the things I felt the first time I laid eyes on her. When we drive over the bridge, conversation is arrested so that nothing detracts from taking in her architecture.

We return to The City later that day or a few days later. We drive along the highway and round the bend. She appears suddenly and never fails to take our breath away.

We say the same thing every single time: *"Whoa this Bridge. This bridge never gets old."*

Just Tell Me

I have many times organized a surprise party for someone important to me.

I delight in every bit of it: the unbelievable display of cunning, the smooth and sleek avoidance of detection, the complex planning, the elaborate plotting, the deep layers of coordination, the awkward, stuttering explanations that despite my most valiant effort make no sense.

Alas, I was not designed for a life of intrigue, stealth and deceit.

Needless to say, if after all this rigamarole someone leaked classified information to the mark — compromising the entire operation — I would be crushed.

Paradoxically, I detest surprises. The feeling of being out of the loop, the sense that something is not adding up, walking into a room where I expected to be alone to be hit with a crowd, then finding myself smack in the middle of a party I am unable to quickly extract myself from (*but Dushka no no you can't leave this is your own party!*). Ack.

Just thinking about it makes me woozy.

Before you engage in the planning of a surprise party make sure you are doing it for someone who would appreciate that kind of effort. And if you know of anyone doing it for me, please.
Just tell me.

No Deep Thoughts

A writer has to sit down and write even on days when she is neither motivated nor inspired. Even on days when she is tired. Even on days when she doesn't know what to write about. Even on days when there is no muse, no enthusiasm, no animated action, no idea, no divine breath.

You shake off the absence of deep thoughts and revelations, ignore the lack of whimsy and vision, crack your knuckles, stretch your neck, pour yourself a cup of coffee, sit down and write.

Why I Love Tacos

Tacos are gently, lovingly folded juicy morsels of flavor.

When I bite into one my mouth experiences nothing less than a tasty explosion of delight.

I close my eyes and rejoice in the simple fact that this delectable, full flavored, mouthwatering scrumptious nosh is all mine.

Then, as I place the very last smidgen, that nibble, that final soupçon into my mouth I know I can always have one more.

And that's why I love tacos.

Oh Yeah

Walking into your office and finding a flower arrangement on your desk.

There is a card under the vase and you haven't opened it but in your mind a person of interest has been identified.

New boots. And oh wow. They are so comfortable.

Mint chocolate chip.

What did I ever do to be this lucky.

I do too. I love you too.

Going to dinner with a friend and longing for four things *OK let's get all of them and share.*

That dress looks really great on you and you want to twirl but you want to be modest, twirl or be modest, make a decision.

Twirl. You twirl.

Reasons Why I Get Up

Breakfast.

Challenging work. Cold water. Feeling useful. The smell of an orange when I peel it. A hot shower. Floating.

Talking to someone new. Date night. Temptation. Ah, so sweet and so grating. Restraint. Life affirming weather. Life affirming sex.

Talking over a meal with just one other person.

Digging into subjects I like. Humans. Relationships. So predictable. So unpredictable. What are we doing?

A new adventure. Feeling off balance. Feeling like I got this. Feeling like I really don't. Surprising myself. Surprising you.

Missing my Dad. Seeing myself in my family. Seeing myself in you.

A starry night. A kiss that will never, ever be. A kiss that can happen any time. A kiss on the nose. Popsicles.

Belting out the lyrics to a good song. Someone joining in. An open window. This feeling that my chest is expanding. My precious good fortune.

Pain. The same mistake, because I am the same person. A good pillow. Getting into bed alone. Cool sheets. Getting into bed with you. Just one kiss. Just one kiss on the nose and then I will let you sleep.

Why Travel When You Can Watch Videos?

A video means I experience places through the eyes of the person taking the video.

When I travel — which is the very best thing I can do with my life, with my time and with my money — I experience things for myself.

I see. Look at this leopard. He was feet away from me, powerful, sinewy, more a liquid than a solid.

I am sorry you can only see a picture because when this picture was taken I could smell him.

I could smell my fear too.

I mean, he could have leaped into my open Jeep and had me for a light snack.

Look at his paws.

I listen. I heard the sound of these elephants crashing out through the trees. They call out to each other. The mom keeps her babies close.

I am sorry you couldn't be there because their beauty and dignity cannot be conveyed with words. It would take your breath away.

It was so hot that day when I was looking at them I could feel my hair matted against my head and sweat trickling down my stomach.

I felt happy to be alive.

I touch.

I go to markets and touch things and smell them and taste them. In this market in Sri Lanka I tasted 7 different kinds of bananas.

I worry that bananas will never be the same. I worry they will never again taste like this, like they did in that market when I was so hot I was actually panting.

I love that heat — like it goes straight into warming my bones.

And I have tried vanilla maybe thousands of times but this glistening vine is something handed to us by a generous god.

And look at all these spices. What a feast. No wonder people navigated to Ceylon braving open waters and a world they thought they might drop off of because they believed it might be flat.

And I have never seen so many perfect flowers, walked through a temple so fragrant with fresh blooms, seen so many people pray and offer these as gifts to Gods and philosophers they believe in.

My senses felt so heightened the hair on my arms and in the back of my neck was raised.

And I saw people light candles and incense hoping for a long life.

When I stepped into this room I reeled back — it was so hot it felt like someone had opened an oven door.

And after days of sweat and heat I swam in a pool of clean water and felt like I was born to swim.

And I often get to sleep in clean, simple, beautiful rooms with smooth sheets and tall pillows.

Please, travel.

Travel to feel, to experience, to revel, to feel devotion, to cry, but mostly travel to understand a simple fact: we are one, my friend.

The things that make us all the same are so much bigger than the ones that make us different.

Get off that comfortable couch where you watch those videos and step outside.

We are one, and if you travel you will see it for yourself.

My Nose

I can tell a lot by smelling a book.

I can tell you if it was just bound or if it's old.

I can tell you if it was loved or forgotten.

I can tell you if it was read many times, passed around, if it was read secretly, or in a way that was rushed or shared or read out loud.

If the previous reader took his time reading while he drank coffee.

I smell books for the same reason I smell people. I like to speculate where they have been before they ended up here with me.

Petrified Wood

One day many years ago I went on a road trip from California to Oregon, along the coast.

It was breathtaking.

I rarely shop for anything, but on this trip I found two things irresistible.

The first was used bookstores. I went into so many. So much happiness for around two dollars each.

I returned home with a box full of books.

The second one was this: along the highway there were many places to buy petrified wood.

It drove me wild. I found it so beautiful. It's so tactile: smooth and scratchy and cold and warm.

After stopping everywhere, seeing everything and petting everything, I bought three.

I kept telling myself there was no good reason to buy them. I mean, what for?

Now I have them in my house and love them so much.

I am sad I didn't get more.

I think I need to make this same road trip again, and get things just because they are beautiful.

Things I Find Beautiful

A big nose.

Passion. Discipline. Dedication. Determination. Ambition.

Competency, at anything.

A good word inserted in the right place in a strong,
short sentence.

An absence of sarcasm.

The guy others deem "too nice".

An ability to see in me what to others is not evident.

A tendency to defy convention, not as a form of rebellion but as
a curious, honest search for identity and happiness.

Taking sides.

Challenging ordinary thinking, even when the ordinary thinking
is mine.

The accidental revolutionary.

The earnest attempt to do the right thing: the textured struggle in
being human and also trying to be good.

Being shown I'm wrong. Not in a way that puts me down, but in a
way that lends me a pair of wings.

Rock Through My Window

Despite a chatty, effervescent exterior, I am intensely introverted, which to me means that most of my life happens inside my head.

I very much enjoy (and seek out) the company of others and believe connection is the meaning of life — at least the meaning of mine. But, being social is something I have to go put on, like an elaborate outfit.

People are work, and interacting always begins with a little bit of dread and takes an enormous expenditure of energy.

Every day I step out of my apartment to run errands or go on a walk and running into someone I know — even someone I love and am happy to see — feels like a disruption, like someone threw a rock through my window.

When I hear *"Dushka!"* I brace myself, then climb over the tall, ivy covered fence of my inner architecture before I am ready to feel excited that I have run into this delightful person.

So, sometimes, (especially if I'm feeling overstimulated) in a desperate search for a shortcut, however clumsy, I notice someone I know and pretend not to see them.

This has nothing to do with them. It has nothing to do with how much I like them. It has to do with me and the fact that my first instinct is to protect my world.

If you see someone and they pretend not to see you, please forgive them. Chances are it has nothing to do with you and that they are thinking about reaching out as soon as they are ready.

What's the Best Song You've Ever Heard?

My yoga teacher occasionally plays a song that makes my heart leap right out of my chest.

All I want is to blast it alone in my living room and dance with complete abandon and in total peace.

The first time I heard it she was talking about the importance of focus and concentration and being fully in the present moment and I just couldn't interrupt *excuse me excuse me what song is that please?*

I didn't hear it again for months and today it came on and she was talking about how we shouldn't rely on external things for our happiness.

Yes yes but

just tell me what song is playing

I need to know.

And I don't know who sings it or what it's called or how it goes and I feel like I spotted a perfect man clear across the room and now I don't know where he went or what his name is or what he was doing here.

To answer your question, I don't know.

I don't know what is the best song I've ever heard.

Real Estate

I've always had intense, vivid, angsty dreams. The past couple of years have made them stranger, more intricate, more epic — a single, large story that spans across years rather than isolated scenes.

World events affect me deeply and seem to seep into my subconscious, giving my dreams a stripped, jagged quality that makes feeling rested nearly impossible.

I have developed an elaborate bedtime ritual to attempt to counteract the effect of my dreams, to give myself the best possible night of sleep. I usually wake up needing to shake something off: an image, or a feeling.

This morning was different.

Last night I dreamed I was looking to buy a house. I visited two open houses and what I saw was disjointed and strange and not right for me.

The real estate agent said that the next house would probably not work. It was bigger than what I needed, and expensive. I said it couldn't hurt to look.

The house was stunning. It was set in the middle of a large garden, and the architecture was open. I walked across the grass and stepped directly into the kitchen (no walls, no doors, no glass).

Then, I walked around the whole place — literally "around" — in a circle. The rooms were separated by the way the furniture was laid out and every room felt intimate and contained despite the absence of enclosures. There was a living room, a bedroom, a library, a sitting room — all sparse and clean in soft, muted colors, mostly cream and gray.

Everything was textured and plush — the grain of different woods, the raw fabric used on the furniture and the thick rugs.

The house was wood, and laid out flat on a single floor, but there was a spiral staircase at the center, intended as a bookcase. It was filled with coffee table books and abstract sculptures. It was the books that filled the house with color.

The light was incredible. The colors, the pattern of the shadows. I wondered how the light could be so intricate if there was no element for it to slant through (no curtains, no windows, no skylights).

I opened my eyes and felt such peace that I was able to experience such a beautiful place.

The dream was so vivid and clear that I wonder if this house exists somewhere, and if so, how I can find it.

(Drawing by Dan Roam, who patiently listened to me attempting to describe something that I can clearly see and not quite articulate.)

Things I Could Write a Poem About

Plum sorbet, a pear, an onion, dust, a trick of the light, water and its glimmer, life and its shades, the way the delicate blouse makes her neck look so graceful, like a dancer.

How you feel when something hurts you, how all you want is to run, and someone else looks at you and says *"You're not crazy. That would hurt me too".*

How you feel when you know you are being incomprehensible, irrational, and someone says *"I understand".*

How you feel when someone wraps you into his arms.

Darkness, anxiety, waking up in the middle of the night feeling like you are in danger.

The last time you packed a suitcase and how even on short trips what you feel is that you are never coming back.

How you can miss a space, your space, like you would miss a person.

The loss, the overwhelming loss of something you never really had. I don't know how I manage to lose so much.

Corn on the cob, roast chicken with red peppers. The red peppers are so good the chicken becomes just a vehicle.

Introducing two people you love and watching the spectacle unfold. They are both here because I told them it was important. This dinner — the food, the light, the temperature, her light blue sandals and his salt and pepper ruffled hair — it's all for me.

Gratitude and how it blooms inside your chest not like a flower but like fire. Like fire.

Strain

Your eyes were made to see.

If they can't see, do you know what they do? They strain.

They strain without you asking them to. They sit there in your eye sockets, straining.

For a long time I have needed glasses to see things that are far away. I needed glasses to drive, to go to the movies, to go to a museum, to walk around the street.

I did not need glasses to read or write or see anything up close.

For the past several months I sit at the computer and wonder what the heck is going on. I push the computer away. I frown and look at it up close. I put lubricating drops into my eyes. I rub them.

It can't be. It can't be that I need glasses for — no.

I finally dragged myself to the eye doctor yesterday.

He sat me down and asked me to look through a big machine with lots of different lenses. He made me look at something far away.

"What feels better, this, or this? Do you prefer view one, or view two? Can you read the first sentence in this sign? What about the last?"

"And what about this piece of paper that's closer?"

"And what about this label, with a print that is nearly microscopic and practically invisible?" (This last sentence might not be a direct quote.)

When he finally arrived at the right prescriptions, I expressed with eloquence how it made me feel: *"Aaaaah yaaaaas. I looooove you."*

I realized then how hard my very dedicated and brave eyes have been working. It was like a sudden, unexpected eye vacation. An eye break. Eye candy.

I now need different sets of glasses for three different activities: to see far away (long distance range). To work at my computer (medium range). To read (close up range).

I'd hate this, but putting them on feels like an eye holiday. Like eye breathing space. Like an eye sabbatical. My eyes, outside enjoying recess.

Without my glasses, my eyes feel burdened. They feel constricted. They are exerted. Exhausted. And I didn't even know.

What's Worse Than Finding a Hair in Your Food?

Back in the day when people went to offices and sat together in crowded conference rooms, we attended a staff meeting where food was ordered for everyone. I don't remember what we were celebrating, but it was a feast.

Big platters of hot food were set across the table, buffet style. Plates and forks and napkins were off to the side so everyone could get everything they needed before sitting down.

We get settled in and tuck into our personal mountains of food.

Suddenly, a woman gets up, puts her hand over her mouth, squeezes her eyes shut and screams. She takes her fork and from her plate flicks a huge cockroach to the center of the conference room table.

It lands right side up and looks huge, intact, inert, complete with long, slender antenna, furry legs and folded wings. It's covered in oily red sauce and has clearly been cooked into the food.

Everyone stands up. Chairs are thrown back. People gag, dry heave, run to the restroom, vacate the room so fast it feels like something just detonated.

A cockroach. That's worse than finding a hair in your food.

Do You Always Know How You Feel?

Are you expecting a word, tight, clean, clear, defined, contained?

Or do you feel like I feel, anxious and tired, drowning in thoughts, tripping over myself, hopeful, exalted?

Are you expecting something like

"Hey sup how are you?"

"Good! Good!"

Or can I say *"wait"*, can I say *"stop, it's been hard, I toss around at night, I'm mostly OK but not always?"*

Thank you for asking — I am thrown off balance, I am always trying to find my feet, and I think this is what it's supposed to be, uncomfortable, an adventure, and I'm excited but also I'm tired. Happy and hurt. Struggling and proud. Motivated and meh. Both yes and no.

I think ya. I do know how I feel. But it's never just one feeling, and it's never something I can explain unless I am granted a bit of time. But yes, nice to see you, and you too. You too have a nice day.

Electric

When I was 14 years old I dreaded going to school. It terrified me to be singled out, to be made fun of, to be ostracized. Saying the wrong thing terrified me. Wearing the wrong socks terrified me.

The amount of energy I expended with my anxiety could have powered a city.

One morning walking to my classroom I noticed at the end of the hall something that stopped me cold. A pile of boys, staring at me. Pointing at me. Laughing. They were holding a piece of paper they kept referring to.

I looked down and slinked over to class.

Later that week I learned what was on that piece of paper because someone taped it to the classroom door. It was a list of all the girls, their physical traits rated on a scale from one to ten.

Some girls cried. Others got angry. Teachers got involved. Parents got involved. Parents with sons said the act was thoughtless but in good fun. Parents with daughters said the act was thoughtless and cruel.

I don't remember exactly how things played out. What I know is that I met up with friends from school decades later — decades.

"That incident has stayed with me," one of them said.

"Those were formative years," said another. *"To this day I still look in the mirror and see a four."*

When I look in the mirror, I see someone generous. I see someone loving. I see someone quick to forgive. I see someone I have to take ferocious good care of, because she has a truly open heart and is easily hurt by others.

Neither you nor I could accurately rate anything about ourselves on a scale from 1 to 10. This is because everything about us — both physical and not — is infinite.

We are limitless, all of us, so pay no mind to anything that distracts you from the fact you could light up a city with the energy expended by the things you do with love.

Green Dress

I have a friend who is a talented painter. When he was young he hung out with other artists and they frequently got drunk or high and created wondrous things.

He felt he was at his best when he was buzzed and got into the habit of sipping and painting through the night, then sleeping all day.

It wasn't just that painting became increasingly frustrating and difficult. It was that the rest of his life began to fall apart. His relationships, his friendships, his health.

He knew he was hooked but the longest hook of all he kept to himself: the awful certainty that the thing he lived for — painting — he could not do when he was sober.

In his mind he wasn't holding on to a habit. He was holding on to his passion. Without it he wasn't sure his life would be worth living.

He would have given everything to continue to paint but his willingness to sacrifice his life was interrupted by his wife who packed her things one day and said she could not continue to be a witness to his destruction.

He attended an AA meeting the next day, mostly to temporarily placate her. Even today he's not sure if he seriously intended to follow through on quitting drinking.

As the fog in his brain receded and he began sleeping through the night he began to feel clearer.

He noticed things he had long forgotten, like the fall of his wife's green dress over her long legs and the fresh flowers she always placed near his easel.

To his utter surprise he began to feel focused again, inspired again, and his ability to paint returned. He was painting more and better than he had in years.

Habits lie. They tell you that what you hold dear you have thanks to them and their voice sounds so much like your own it can take years for you to tell the difference.

Forget happy

By Dushka Zapata

I don't know about you, but for
me the holidays are not "happy."

Holidays can feel like there is no floor and I don't know how long the fall is going to be.

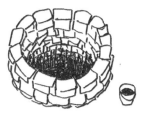

I wish happiness came easy, rather than something forced upon me.

But all I hear is have a happy this or have a happy that. All I hear is cheer.

My gift to myself is realizing that it's okay to not be happy. My gift to myself is knowing there is nothing wrong with me.

It's ok to curl up inside myself,
to let the days be long and quiet.

If the holidays don't make you
happy, defend your right to feel
whatever you're feeling.

This to me is the real gift of the holiday season. The space I grant myself to be abstracted or pensive or moody or, yes, even scared.

By giving myself this space, instead of feeling out of step with the world, I feel in step with me.

You Smell Good

Bread baking in the oven, fresh cut grass, thinner and oil paints, clay and Play-Doh.

Tide (the detergent). Tide was ubiquitous in Mexico and the smell remained on the clothes of anyone who hugged or held me.

Chlorine — the smell of a sparkling clean house and also the smell of swimming pools, which have always been and will always be one of my favorite places.

Bubble gum — the pink one, and the grape one.

Meat on the grill. Whiskey, tequila and beer which I could smell on the breath of loving adults who looked after me and kissed the top of my head.

Later, cigarettes, Drakkar Noir and Acqua Di Gio, rum and coke. New car smell and fireworks.

The smell of gasoline when it went into a car or a motorcycle, the smell of pavement on a tarmac and the smell of the Pacific Ocean, which I've pursued. A good life lived by following my nose.

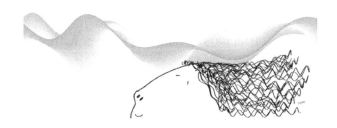

Welcome Back

One of my oldest friends is an absolute force of nature, larger than life, magnificent.

In my (clearly completely unbiased) opinion she has always been gorgeous, but when anyone comments on that she shrugs it off. "*Other things matter more,*" she's always said. "*Tell me what you stand for.*"

Through all the time I've known her she has made it a point to deposition beauty. Like it's too superficial a characteristic to be worthy of her time.

A few years ago she was struck by depression. She went from having an outrageous personality to becoming a shell.

I found her unrecognizable. She was hollow and indifferent, as if someone had reached into her chest with a closed fist and turned off the light.

During one of my visits, a common friend arrived accompanied by a professional makeup artist. I thought to myself, *"After years of friendship it's like you don't know her at all".*

I felt protective but recognized she was brimming with love and the best of intentions so, in a rare display of prudence, I kept my big mouth shut.

The professional make-up artist had a gentle soul. She walked over to our friend like she was approaching a startled wild animal. She spoke in a soft, soothing voice, got closer, asked if she could look at her. She put her finger on her chin and turned her face left and right. She touched her hair.

Then she took her hand and walked her over to the bathroom.

She colored her hair. She gave her a facial, a manicure and a pedicure. She applied makeup and did her hair up in a chignon. She looked through her closet, pulled out a simple gown and asked her to put it on. Then she walked her over to a full-length mirror.

I want to cry thinking of the way she reacted to her own reflection. It was like she had forgotten who she was and she had just recovered the ability to remind herself. She stared. She turned. She swiveled. She strutted back and forth.

It would be preposterous for me to suggest that this makeover cured her depression. But I can tell you it played a role in returning to her the person she had lost touch with, the person everyone but her could see.

Persimmons and Pomegranates

Persimmons — crunchy, bright orange persimmons that remind me of a cross between a pumpkin and an apple; and pomegranates, that are almost too beautiful to eat.

My man and I sit at the table in my kitchen and he takes a sharp knife and cuts the pomegranate into sections, then divides and places them onto two colorful bowls. We sit and talk and crunch on the seeds that look like jewels.

We can't do anything else — can't grab a notebook or a computer or our phones — because our fingers and hands are covered in pomegranate juice.

Pomegranates hold us hostage with their beauty and their succulence and all we can do is talk, look at each other, catch up on our day, and dream (which is our way of planning).

We dream, but sitting here all peaceful and engrossed in this pomegranate, talking to the most interesting person I have ever met, I already feel like I have everything.

Movies Always Get This Wrong

Whenever a character has done something that requires him (or her) to vanish into thin air, whenever the script demands a lawless, anarchic, barbarous, crude, uncouth location, the character escapes to…

Mexico.

People. Civilization does not abruptly end beyond US borders.

How Do You Come Up With Ideas To Write About?

I have a friend who loves to paint. He spends time at art supply stores, walks down every aisle, runs his hands over the different colors in every shade. He buys tubes of paint and canvases and stashes them in his small apartment.

He has an easel in the middle of his living room, and there is always a painting in progress on it, another leaning against the wall.

When I go on walks with him, he interrupts conversations to stop and take pictures. Or he'll stop dead in his tracks and gasp. *"Dushka,"* he will say. *"Look at the light."*

"I love the color of your rain jacket. Look, how it matches this wall of graffiti. Please, just stand there. I need to photograph this."

I never wonder how he manages to come up with ideas on what to paint. He sees future paintings everywhere.

Even if he had time to paint them all, he'd have a new truckload of ideas by early tomorrow. Because, look at this wall of graffiti, and the color of your jacket, how everything looks completely different in the early morning light.

Would You Agree To Have a Tail in Exchange for a Billion Dollars?

My tail would be pure muscle. It would be so substantial it would give me propulsive force, both on land and on water.

I could lie on my back on the surface of a lake, languid, and stretch out my arms and legs, using just a relaxed, gentle swish of my tail to check out the surroundings.

I'd use it to lean on whenever I had to stand in line at the airport.

With my tail I would be able to lift myself off the ground to get a better view at vista points. I'd swoosh it left and right to release all my pent up enthusiasm, being careful not to thwack someone with it.

My tail would be so strong that if you gave me good news or shared something beautiful with me, like a poem or a sketch, you'd hear it thumping from blocks away. Snuggling would include longitudinal tail-scratchies.

My tail would be covered with a silky, curly haired coat. On Sunday afternoons you'd find me at home wearing a coconut oil/rose water hair and tail treatment. Both my hair and my tail would be glossy, healthy and lustrous.

I would sleep peacefully, with my mighty tail wrapped around me, for warmth and for safety.

Things That Amaze Me

Coffee. Breakfast. Food. The ineffable expression in his eyes. I don't think I will ever tire of looking at them.

Hot water, and how I feel after a shower, like I switched from my body into a newer one.

Floating, and how I feel after floating, like I switched from my brain into a new one.

Human adaptability, so ferocious. I love it. You are incredible, and resilient.

A clear blue sky after a day of rain. Rain after good weather. Wind, whipping my hair around. Sex.

A good conversation, like a never ending labyrinth, all pleasure.

The fact that nothing is ever predictable or safe. All the things we refuse to see to convince ourselves that it is.

Grief, and how it still bolts through me as if he had died only yesterday.

The fact that he is always, always with me, and how I know his loss is not real.

Kissing. Popcorn. Popsicles. Belting out the lyrics to a song and someone joining in — the shock of sudden belonging.

A window that opens wide. Sun that streams in. Light that streams in.

That feeling that my chest is expanding. The fleeting sense that everything is connected. The sense, less fleeting, that I am inestimably fortunate.

A good pillow. Clean, cool sheets. A well-made bed, symmetrical and tucked in tight at the corners. The *aaaah* of crawling into one at the end of a long day. The *aaaah* of crawling into one several hours earlier than normal, because one of the joys of being an adult is that I am the decider of "bedtime".

Grainy mustard. A jasmine plant that I walk by at night. The right word in the right place.

Writing.

Lessons From the 2020 Lockdown

I am more introverted than I thought.

Days go by fast.

I do better with a routine than without one.

I've become better at taking things one day at a time.

I've become better at living in the present.

Anything I've become better at I've done because I've been practicing.

I remind myself to treat myself with compassion. No beating myself up over what I'm doing or what I'm not.

It feels good to tell people how I feel.

I begin and end every conversation with thank you and I love you. I can't ever say either of those things too much.

It's very important for me to move. After an online yoga class or a walk I feel much better.

Beautiful things make me feel grounded and connected to where I've been and what I've done. I don't really have expensive things. I have meaningful things, and I'm very grateful for them.

There are many things I told myself I didn't do because I didn't have time but it turns out I don't do them even when I do have time.

I am a lot less anxious when I have real reasons to feel uncertain.

Nobody Knows

I spend most of my energy exercising restraint.

I am a happy person who suffers from regular, nearly unbearable bouts of existential angst.

I suffer from anxiety.

I never sleep through the night.

I am always heartbroken.

I worry about the things I am not doing — mostly the people I love I am not spending time with.

There are many things about me that I have never told anyone but it's more because of privacy than because of secrecy.

My writing comes from the fact that I am hurting. Nearly everything I write was originally designed for me to feel lighter, better, more at peace, to ease the things I describe above. They work for me most of the time and I share them because I hope they do the same for you.

Supermarket

I went to the supermarket twice today. I wanted to put myself in a position where I'd need to leave my house as little as possible, because we are in the middle of a pandemic and it's the responsible thing to do — not just for me but for those around me.

In my first supermarket visit, the shelves that carried cans, crackers, and toilet paper looked empty. It stunned me.

People around me were clearly on edge. Stressed, anxious, haphazardly grabbing things from shelves and throwing them into their carts.

I wanted to buy dishwasher detergent and there was one left but I couldn't reach it. I suddenly felt a sense of powerlessness rise inside of me.

That's when I saw that the box I had been reaching for was right in front of my eyes. I took it, then realized a very tall person was handing it to me.

"It looks like you wanted this, yes?" he says this to me very gently.

I turn and we just stand there looking at each other, a pause in the middle of a frenzy spinning around us. He smiles at me. His smile feels like someone just dropped a sturdy anchor in the middle of a turbulent ocean.

The times we are living in are surreal. Please, stop and be nice to someone.

Arbitrary

Have you ever given any thought to what happens after "happily ever after?"

"Happily ever after" does not mark the end, but the beginning of a relationship.

All stories — including our own — are never ending. We just cut them off in arbitrary places to better grasp the world around us.

My Summary

Writer.

Perfect stranger. Recovering overachiever. Language lover. Periodic insomniac. Kinetic. Sensory. Clutter-phobic. Faith full agnostic.

Voraciously curious. Invincibly happy.

A Bit More

Dushka Zapata has worked in communications for over twenty years, running agencies (such as Edelman and Ogilvy) and working with companies to develop their corporate strategy.

During this time she specialized in executive equity and media and presentation training. She helped people communicate better through key message refinement and consistency and coached them to smoothly manage difficult interviews with press during times of crisis.

Dushka is an executive coach and public speaker who imparts workshops about personal brand development. She has been hired for strategic alignment hiring, to coach and mentor high potential individuals, improve upon new business pitches, refine existing processes and galvanize a company's communication efforts.

She recently built and ran the communications team at Zendesk; then became head of communications for Forte, a start up that believes games can unlock new economic opportunities for billions of people.

She now runs executive communications for Game7, a DAO formed to accelerate the adoption of Web3 Gaming.

Dushka is the author of fifteen books: "How to be Ferociously Happy", "Amateur: an inexpert, inexperienced, unauthoritative, enamored view of life", "A Spectacular Catastrophe and other things I recommend", "Your Seat Cushion is a Flotation Device and other buoyant short stories", "Someone Destroyed My Rocket Ship and other havoc I have witnessed at the office", "How to Build a Pillow Fort and other valuable life lessons", "You Belong Everywhere and other things you'll have to see for yourself", "Love Yourself and other insurgent acts that recast everything", "Feelings Are Fickle and other things I wish someone had told me", "How to Draw Your Boundaries and why no one else can save you", "The Love of Your Life Is You: A Step-

By-Step Workbook to Loving Yourself", " Demote Yourself and other ways to show your ego who's boss", "For All I Know: a shebang of checklists for life", "Please Don't Blame Love: a relationship handbook", and the one you have in your hands.

Dushka was named one of the top 25 innovators in her industry by The Holmes Report and regularly contributes to Quora, the question and answer site, where she has nearly 300 million views.

About the Illustrator

Dan Roam is the author of six international bestselling books on visual storytelling. **The Back of the Napkin** was named by Fast Company, The London Times, and BusinessWeek as the "Creativity Book of the Year".

Dan is a creative director, author, painter, and model-builder. His purpose in life is to make complex things clear by drawing them and to help others do the same. Dan has helped leaders at Allbirds, Google, Microsoft, Boeing, Gap, IBM, the US Navy, and the Obama White House solve complex problems with simple pictures.

Dan and his whiteboard have appeared many times on CNN, MSNBC, ABC, CBS, Fox, and NPR.

Author's Note

I hope you liked my book!

If you have questions about anything along the way, or want to explore any subject I write about, I suggest you enter my name and any key word in the Quora search window. This way you can find everything I've written about what you seek, and maybe come across other helpful things along the way.

You can also post comments and questions on Instagram, using the hashtag #dushkazapatateacupstories.

If you like my short stories, I've written other books that collect them: "Amateur: an inexpert, inexperienced, unauthoritative, enamored view of life", "Your Seat Cushion is a Flotation Device and other buoyant short stories", "You Belong Everywhere and other things you'll have to see for yourself", and "How To Be Ferociously Happy and other essays".

Remember that everything I write — including all of the content of the books I mention above — is available on Quora for free.

If you find any of this helpful or enjoyable, please write Amazon reviews so that other people can find them too.

Dushka Zapata

San Francisco, California

November 2023

Made in the USA
Las Vegas, NV
24 November 2023